I GIVE MYSELF PERMISSION

Take Risks. Be Imperfect. Live Boldly.

George James, PsyD, LMFT

New Harbinger Publications, Inc.

Publisher's Note

NEW HARBINGER PUBLICATIONS is a registered
trademark of New Harbinger Publications, Inc.

New Harbinger Publications is an employee-owned company.

Copyright © 2026 by George James
        New Harbinger Publications, Inc.
        5720 Shattuck Avenue
        Oakland, CA 94609
        www.newharbinger.com

Cover design by Sara Christian

Interior design by Michele Waters-Kermes

Acquired by Jed Bickman

Edited by Karen Schader

Library of Congress Cataloging-in-Publication Data on file

Printed in the United States of America

28   27   26

10   9   8   7   6   5   4   3   2   1   First Printing

"I've had the pleasure of working with Dr. George James, and he helped me grow and understand both the journey I was on and the one ahead. It was a real honor to get his perspective—and to learn how to give myself permission to face the different battles I was juggling, especially when they became overwhelming. I wouldn't have the patience or mental strength I have today without the Doc's help."

—**Danny Green**, three-time NBA Champion, TV analyst, and host of the *Inside the Green Room with Danny Green* podcast

"I've often wished I could get advice from Dr. George James every day—he's just that special. *I Give Myself Permission* is that very gift. Practical, compassionate, and wise, this is a book you'll return to again and again."

—**Savannah Sellers**, NBC News anchor of *Morning News Now*, NBC News correspondent, and cohost of *Stay Tuned*

"What if the biggest obstacle to your success is the permission you haven't given yourself? *I Give Myself Permission by George James* is a powerful guide to breaking free from self-imposed limitations—fear, perfectionism, and past trauma—and stepping fully into the life you deserve. Drawing from real stories, practical exercises, and deep insights, this book will help you move beyond what's holding you back and take action toward your true potential."

—**Shaka Senghor**, *New York Times* bestselling author of *Writing My Wrongs*, *Letters to the Sons of Society*, and *How to Be Free*

"In *I Give Myself Permission*, Dr. George James offers a powerful, compassionate guide to overcoming fear and self-doubt, helping readers break free from the barriers holding them back. With practical tools and inspiring insights, this book empowers you to embrace your unique path and take the bold steps needed to live a life aligned with who you really are."

—**Elizabeth Earnshaw, LMFT**, therapist, entrepreneur, and author of *I Want This to Work* and *'Til Stress Do Us Part*

"*I Give Myself Permission* is a masterpiece! Powered by professional expertise and fueled by unyielding faith, this book provides us with the tools necessary to live our best lives and become our best selves. Read it and prepare to be transformed."

—**Marc Lamont Hill, PhD**, author, professor, TV host, and cohost of the *Joe Budden Podcast*

"Dr. George James is an incredibly rare mix—a deeply experienced therapist and an executive coach working with some of the most powerful leaders in the world. He's also just a kind, thoughtful friend whom I've turned to for advice for over a decade. I can't recommend this book enough. It's a guide to starting your next, powerful chapter, whether you're a Fortune 100 exec or a stay-at-home parent doing your best to hold it all together."

—**Melissa Hobley**, global chief marketing officer at Tinder

"In *I Give Myself Permission*, Dr. George James empowers readers to break free from limitations and step boldly into their fullest potential. With deep insight and practical guidance, he challenges us to dream big, take risks, and release the fears that hold us back. Through powerful stories and actionable strategies, this book serves as a road map to self-discovery and personal transformation. A must-read for anyone ready to embrace their true calling and create a life of purpose and fulfillment."

—**Paul C. Brunson**, TV host of *Married at First Sight UK* and *Celebs Go Dating*, host of the *We Need To Talk* podcast, relationship expert, entrepreneur, and author

"*I Give Myself Permission* is, in a word, transformational. It's pushed me to evolve in every area of my life—to change my mindset, habits, and behaviors to not just survive, but thrive. This book is the antidote to what's holding so many people back from becoming their best selves and living fully."

—**Leonard Hammonds II**, director of leadership communities at the nonprofit BMe Community, US Marine Corps veteran, and founder of Hammonds Initiative

"Dr. George James' *I Give Myself Permission* offers a powerful blueprint for breaking free—from perfectionism, family scripts, and self-limiting beliefs—and stepping into the bold, authentic life you were always meant to live. This is a must-read for anyone ready to stop holding themselves back and finally become the fulfilled, grounded, and empowered version of themselves they know they can be."

—**BJ Johnson**, assistant general manager of the Brooklyn Nets, entrepreneur, real estate developer, and investor

"In a world that teaches us to look outward for happiness, it's not always obvious that everything we need is already inside of us. With this book, Dr. George James helps us reframe that idea of access—and shows how the simple act of giving ourselves permission can help us unlock our deepest desires."

—**Stephanie Humphrey**, nationally syndicated technology contributor and author

"Having known Dr. James for years, I've experienced firsthand how his wisdom and compassion have positively shaped my life. His words—and his unwavering commitment to helping others—shine through in this book, and will undoubtedly have a powerful impact on everyone who reads it."

—**Toney Goins**, actor in *Billions* and *For Life*

"Dr. George James has a rare gift for guiding people through fear, self-doubt, and the weight of the past. *I Give Myself Permission* is a powerful road map to healing, courage, and real transformation. This book will inspire you to give yourself permission to grow, to forgive, and to step fully into the life you're meant to live."

—**Leon Ford**, cofounder of The Hear Foundation, author of *An Unspeakable Hope*, social entrepreneur, impact investor, international speaker, and changemaker

"Dr. George James has written a gem for anyone ready to step into meaningful change. His warm, engaging style and thoughtful questions spark deep self-reflection, helping readers break through limiting beliefs. The real-talk insights and vulnerable storytelling create an immediate sense of connection, offering both inspiration and practical steps forward. Treat yourself to the gift of I Give Myself Permission—it will leave you feeling seen, encouraged, and ready to grow."

>—**Daria Torres**, managing partner at Walls Torres Group, and lecturer at The Wharton School of the University of Pennsylvania

To my parents, Gwendolyn and George James

Thank you for all your sacrifices, love, and faith. Miss you both!

and

To my wife and children, whose endless love and support inspire me daily

Contents

The Stories We Tell Ourselves

*We are all story. We are the stories we
are told, and we are the stories we tell
ourselves. To change our circumstances,
we need to change our story: edit it,
modify it, or completely rewrite it.*

—Harold R. Johnson

What's the last song that was stuck in your head? Maybe it was the latest tune from Taylor Swift or Beyoncé, a classic from Bob Marley or Marc Anthony, a song from the *Hamilton* soundtrack, or your favorite from a movie or television show. You probably bobbed your head, hummed, danced, or even sang it out loud. Songs can get stuck in our head on repeat.

That's how our personal story can be. It's an earworm, too. We tell and retell our story about who we are, who we aren't, how we "should" be, and what we "should" do. The details begin to take shape at an early age, and throughout our lifetime, our story solidifies, for better or for worse.

Of course, just like any good book or movie, the details of who you are and the character you play in the story also develop over time. Take Harry Potter, for instance, in the beginning of the first book, *Harry Potter and the Sorcerer's Stone*. We learn that he's an eleven-year-old orphan who is being mistreated by his relatives. He has little confidence in himself, but he's clever and soon learns that he's a wizard. By the last book, *Harry Potter and the Deathly Hallows*, he knows his strengths and challenges. He has won some battles and lost some, and he has made lifelong friends.

As the reader, or the viewer of the movies, we may believe different things about Harry than he believes about himself. For example, Dumbledore has faith in Harry, while Professor Snape puts him down. Sometimes the people around us hold beliefs about us and our abilities that differ from our own beliefs. They might perceive strengths we don't give ourselves credit for, or they might perceive weaknesses that don't exist.

Over the years, our story can be shaped by many factors, such as how involved our parents were in our life or if we did well in school, sports, theater, or music. Interactions with siblings, friends, and romantic partners have an impact, as well as our physical and mental health history, level of education, experiences with death, divorces, triumphs, and tragic moments.

These factors are data points in the story you tell yourself about yourself and in the story that's told to you *about you* by others. It's either explicit (said directly to you about what you can or can't do, sometimes based on little to no evidence) or implicit (subliminal or subtle messages that have come to you through people, books, television, movies, music, and social media).

This story in your head directly shapes what you believe is possible for you. It shapes your career, who you select as a partner, and what you do in life, including hobbies, decisions, behaviors, travel, sports, habits, courses of study, and more. It even affects your ability to have fun, rest, and take breaks.

Your story can reverberate through your mind and emotions on replay (just like that earworm), even when no one else is around. And it can limit you in many areas of your life. After all, we're inundated with obligations and stressors, both personal and collective, that lead us to impose unnecessary limitations on ourselves. Often, we give up on our aspirations and settle for lesser options than what we want or need. Without realizing it, we put ourselves in a box full of limits, believing what we hope to do or want to stop doing isn't possible. At times, we even say, in our minds, that the thing, the idea, the opportunity is not possible for us and is possible for others.

This was the case for my client, Ron, who was forty years old when he started therapy with me. "I feel like such a failure at everything," he announced during our first session. "My fiancé broke up with me. I keep applying for new jobs, but I'm not getting any interviews. I feel stuck."

As we started to talk about his childhood, Ron revealed that his father constantly disappointed him. His dad would frequently promise to pick him up from his mother's house and then fail to show up. This repeated experience led him to create an internal narrative that his wants and desires weren't important and would never be fulfilled. Because of this storyline, he grew up trying to never get his hopes up. Even though he was intelligent, he felt defeated, so he didn't give his all in his classes, which led him to barely graduate from high school.

Still, as much as Ron tried to avoid being disappointed, another part of him fought back and kept trying. In our first session, I was able to reframe what he had always seen as failures. For example, until I pointed out that he was someone who refused to quit, he was unaware of it. I helped him see that he never gave up, especially with his education. After leaving high school with a grade point average under 2.0, he worked hard to get into college, got accepted to law school (even though he chose not to pursue that path), and as of the writing of this book, has earned not one, but *two* master's degrees and become fluent in Spanish. How does that in any way make him a failure? Yet even though his casting himself as a failure wasn't true, that's the story that had been the earworm in his head since childhood.

Despite his accomplishments and tenaciousness, Ron struggled to pursue his talent and passion to become a writer. Due to that old story, he wrestled with insecurity and a fear of failure, believing no one would want to read his work. Again, he didn't want to be disappointed, so he struggled to start.

During our time together, I continued to reframe Ron's negative inner story as I had done on the first day. Eventually, he started to integrate a new story that allowed him to give himself more permission in his life. This story helped him realize that it wasn't about the outcome of who would read his writing. It was about not limiting himself and instead living his life boldly on his own terms, not based on the pain of his past that had written a false story in his mind.

There were many starts, stops, and "almosts" throughout the process, but Ron gave himself permission to try. This mindset now permeates his life. He now says, "I will try. I will give myself permission." He's writing now with hopes of publishing one day and has also started a podcast.

It wasn't easy for Ron to give himself permission to pursue his dream, but that's what each of us must learn to do. We have to learn how to give ourselves permission *beyond the false story we've been telling ourselves throughout our life.*

You may find that, like Ron, you've been putting yourself down with a negative story, and you may have struggled to pursue certain dreams or desires. This book is about discovering that the story you've always believed about yourself may not be true after all. And it doesn't *have* to be true if it isn't what you want. You can do as Ron did and integrate a new story that allows you to take risks, be imperfect, live boldly, and fulfill your full potential for achievement, enjoyment, and self-care. You, too, can give yourself permission to be who you want to be and do what you want to do with your life.

Why a Therapist?

Of course, I have my own personal experience with giving myself permission.

I grew up in a family and culture that didn't talk about psychology or mental health, so how on earth did I end up becoming a therapist? How did I push past the subtle, and sometimes overt, messages I received about therapy? The subtle ones included that it wasn't a viable career option. After all, I didn't see people in the profession who looked like me (Black men specifically). The overt messages were that talking about your feelings makes you weak, that we should "just pray about it," and "what happens at home is our business and stays at home." How, in the midst of all of this, did I give myself permission to become a therapist?

Well, for many years, I thought I wanted to become a medical doctor. My parents often shared that when I was just five years old, I said, "I want to be a doctor like Aunty Clover!" She was a close family friend and my closest relationship with a physician.

That desire to become a doctor continued until the end of my sophomore year of college. Unfortunately, my science grades weren't nearly as high as my other grades. And when I truly examined the lifestyle of a medical doctor, it really didn't appeal to me.

But the story in my head was that if I became a doctor, my parents would be proud, and if I didn't, they'd be disappointed. This narrative almost kept me stuck because I felt like shifting my major would be equivalent to failing my family. That wasn't true, but I had convinced myself it was. The *actual* truth was that the only person I was failing was myself for not following what was right for me, and I made myself miserable in the process.

What I started to realize was that, throughout my life, I have always wanted to help people. Seeing my parents help others in the community, sometimes giving their all even when they didn't have a lot to offer, set a meaningful example for me. In college, I naturally gravitated to clubs that were proactive in helping other students on campus.

After many prayers, several conversations with professors, and a frank and difficult talk with my parents, I was able to give myself permission to change my major from biology to psychology. This change led me to the path of my dreams, filled with purpose and fulfillment. Eventually, I continued on to graduate school in psychology to learn how to become a therapist.

All of these moments filled with desire, purpose, and ambition have helped me become the therapist, executive coach, consultant to family-owned businesses, and international speaker that I am today. I wouldn't be here if I hadn't admitted to myself that my initial path in medicine wasn't a good fit and then given myself permission to do something else.

I have long been interested in what gets people stuck and what keeps them stuck. I'm fascinated by the reasons we struggle to pursue our aspirations and what we tend to give up as we pursue other goals. Some people give themselves permission in one area, for example, while ignoring other areas of their life. In my clinical practice, I have wanted to learn more about the stories people repeat to themselves and how those stories can create lifelong limitations. That fascination, study, and work with my clients has led to the writing of this book.

The Practical and Deep Seesaw

In total, I have been practicing for over twenty-four years and have had over twelve years of higher education, including my undergraduate studies, and add to that my own lived experience. When I first started doing therapy, I thought every session and every client had to have a deep emotional breakthrough. Many of my clients also had this thought. Maybe this was due to many examples on television and in pop culture that make it seem like therapy can change your life in one master class.

As a result, I gravitated to theories that looked at family history and family dynamics to help explain current (and sometimes future) behavior. I used theories like the Bowen family systems model (Kerr and Bowen 1988), which emphasizes how our behavior is often repeated and similar to our family and the multigenerational experiences before us. A key aspect of Bowen's theory is *differentiation of self*, which is a process where one is able to acknowledge influence from others while also being able to think and feel on their own. To ensure that we are able to think and feel on our own, it is important that we are doing the work of examining ourselves, acknowledging how others influence us, and finding our true self, somewhere between complete independence from others and dependence on others. This theory and others guided me in helping my clients explore deeper, more insightful aspects of their current condition.

As I became more seasoned, however, I realized that some clients needed help making changes more quickly. They didn't want the insight or the family perspective. They just wanted to understand how they could shift, adjust, and change *now*. I used approaches like cognitive behavioral therapy (CBT) to coach my clients through the connection between their thoughts, feelings, and behaviors. This approach was more practical, and many of my clients appreciated the ability to get right to the issue.

These experiences shaped my overall clinical experience, enabling me to provide practical solutions, interventions, and methods while also integrating deeper, more insightful explorations. I moved from an either-or to a both-and approach to my work.

In guiding people to explore where they need to give themselves permission or where they have challenges in giving themselves permission, I use both practical and deep perspectives. For example, some people can easily ask their boss for the day off, while others find it difficult. And we need to understand why it's so difficult for us. What part of our history is connected to our difficulty in asking for a day off? Or simply taking a day off for those who have autonomy in their work schedules? Once we have that insight and awareness, we can begin to shift whatever our inner story is telling us about taking a day off and give ourselves permission to do it. Practically, this includes looking at our calendars and choosing a day you want off, then asking for (or taking) that day off.

This combination of insight-based work and practical work led me to narrative therapy (White and Epston 1990) and the importance of our stories. Our internal narratives are linked to the pain, challenges, and messages from our past, and they influence the decisions we make in our present. Throughout this book, I will invite you to examine your internal narrative by reflecting on influences from your past (family, culture, community) and decisions you make or don't make in the present.

The Context Matters

I believe that there are other aspects of life besides the ones I already mentioned that shape who we are and how we show up in life. These variables are a part of our life experiences and can influence how we see the world and how the world sees us, and I would be remiss to leave them out.

These contextual aspects play some role for most people, and for some, they play a vital role in their internal and external worldview. These variables can influence how hard or how easy it is to give yourself permission in particular areas. Each category can provide opportunities for privilege/advantage or for oppression/injustice, depending on what identity or identities you have. These variables that influence life experiences may include (but certainly are not limited to) race, ethnicity, class, age, gender, sexual identity, faith, ability, and history of trauma. In addition, the intersection of these identities, called intersectionality, can create a more layered and sometimes complex experience for people.

Just bear this factor in mind as you consider the challenges that you have experienced in your life.

Where Do You Need to Give Yourself Permission?

As you continue reading, this book will guide you through multiple places where you can explore giving yourself permission to start, stop, push further, or try something else. At some points, you will be asked to write down your thoughts or responses to questions, and you will have the option of using your journal or downloading the material at my website—www.IGiveMyselfPermission.com/downloads. There will be deeper reflections to examine your blocks and the areas where you feel stuck—areas such as why it has been so difficult for you to let go of a multiyear relationship that isn't bringing out the best in you or why you haven't yet gotten the EIN for your new business. You will explore the story you tell about yourself and begin to write a new one for the new life you will give yourself permission to have.

Congratulations on starting your permission journey. As you begin this path of reflection, examination, and action, it will be important to determine what additional support you need to help you fully change your narrative. Do you need to go to a seminar, work with a coach, start or continue therapy, journal, or something else? Figuring out what you need to stay consistent with the changes is called doing the work.

I encourage you to do the work and use this book as a resource to help you take risks, be imperfect, let go of limitations, embrace vulnerability, and live boldly.

Chapter 1

Barriers to Permission

I always did something I was a little not ready to do. I think that's how you grow. When there's that moment of "Wow, I'm not really sure I can do this," and you push through those moments, that's when you have a breakthrough.

—Marissa Mayer

Gwendolyn James, my mother, had a thirty-three-year career as a patient care associate (formerly known as a nurse's aide) at Englewood Hospital Medical Center. Prior to that she supported the Brown family, who sponsored her citizenship after she migrated to the United States from Jamaica. She was a spiritual woman and a leader in the church. Her time was split between working, church, and family. For most of her career, she worked the night shift, typically 11:00 p.m. to 7:00 a.m. Sometimes she worked a double shift to get overtime.

On the weekends, she would go to work on Saturday night and come home Sunday morning. Once she arrived home, she would make breakfast and go to church with the family. She would be at church for most of the day, at least six hours, before returning home. Somehow, she mustered enough energy to cook dinner and entertain guests. Then she would take a short nap and go back to work for another night shift.

I witnessed this chain of events week after week, month after month, year after year. In the moments when she wasn't working, I often watched her fall asleep at the kitchen table. She didn't take vacations either—even though she wanted to travel the world.

Early in her career, she had the opportunity to become a nurse, but she needed a high school diploma or equivalent. She took her GED exam and missed the passing mark by only a few points. My mother often shared that she always wanted to go back to retake her exam, but she never did it.

This amazing, thoughtful, caring, spiritual, kind, and hardworking woman sacrificed so much for her family and countless others. At the same time, she didn't give herself permission to do the things she loved or needed. She didn't give herself permission to travel the world, advance her career, rest, or put her needs before the needs of others.

Privilege of Permission

Giving yourself permission is a privilege. Many people wish they could give themselves permission, but due to their circumstances, they feel they can't. Maybe you can't take a day off because you need the money or your request for vacation time was rejected, forcing you to work. Some people might have to work multiple jobs or overtime to make ends meet. You could be caring for your parents while taking care of your own children, balancing your needs while loving your child who has learning differences or special needs. Or getting around might include multiple buses, trains, or the cost of ride services, like Uber and Lyft. You could be a single parent raising your children on a salary that barely makes ends meet, or part of a young couple overwhelmed with student loans and credit card debt, or a family dealing with illness and medical debt. Continuous obstacles get in the way and overwhelm you, making you believe that permission is something other people can give themselves...but not you.

Yet the narrative that people "like you" can't give yourselves permission—that if you had more money, you could give yourself permission is false. Yes, you have real challenges, and there are different types of privileges unique to each individual. When there's a lot of stress and worry, it's particularly hard to think about permission. But even with those challenges, everyone can find a way to give themselves *more* permission. Whatever your circumstances are, don't count yourself out.

Yes, there is privilege in being able to wake up one day and give yourself permission to take a mental health day, leave your job, go back to school, spend the day with your child or grandchild instead of checking emails, or start the business you've been dreaming about. But giving yourself permission could also be asking for help, volunteering in an industry you are passionate about, or taking one course at a time over years until you get enough credits to graduate. Everyone can give themselves permission—it just might look a little different for each individual, depending on their circumstances.

My mother didn't think she could give herself permission to travel, take breaks, and practice self-care because she often put others first. Although this was one of her amazing qualities, it also got in the way of her ability to fully enjoy her life. Giving herself permission felt like a privilege that she didn't have, but I wish she had known that everyone has that right.

The Top Four Barriers to Permission

Some of the reasons my mother didn't give herself permission are the same reasons why you and I struggle to give ourselves permission. In fact, these include the top four barriers I have heard from my clients and audience members at my keynote talks and seen in my work over the years. Throughout this book, I'll provide many examples of giving yourself permission, and I'll offer encouraging suggestions for how to do it. At the same time, I don't want you to believe that all you have to do is say the magic words, "I give myself permission," and click your heels, and everything will be fine.

There are internal and external barriers that make giving yourself permission challenging. The four main barriers I have observed are (1) social stress, (2) leadership stress, (3) injustice stress, and (4) family of origin stress.

Barrier #1: Social Stress

Stress is all around us. In a survey conducted by the American Dental Association (ADA) Health Policy Institute (2021), over 70 percent of dentists surveyed said that they saw an increase in stress-related dental conditions, such as teeth grinding. The previous survey had reported that less than 60 percent of dentists witnessed stress-related teeth grinding. Members of the ADA Health Policy Institute have attributed this increase to the onset of Covid-19 and the subsequent stressors that have occurred since then.

But there are so many social stressors that we don't actively pay attention to them. We go on with our day, thinking about what we have to do, and we ignore these stressors until we're forced to deal with them. How much do you avoid breaking news, eat more than you normally do (or previously did), cry in your car before you enter the house, get in an argument with someone even though they aren't the source of your frustration, or go to bed hoping the pain will go away?

Unfortunately, the act of suppressing the impact of these stressors also makes us suppress our ability to give ourselves permission. It's almost impossible to heal from the barrage of stressors if we don't acknowledge that they are present and have an effect. As psychologist Carl Jung (2003) said, "Until you make the unconscious conscious, it will direct your life, and you will call it fate." These social stressors are directing our lives and the choices we make, including giving ourselves permission.

This next part might be uncomfortable, but it's a necessary step to giving yourself permission. The list that follows presents topics that are typical stressors in our lives. Take your time looking at these topics and ask yourself: on a scale of 1 to 10—with 10 being the highest and 1 being the lowest—what is your stress level in each category?

Next, take out your journal and write down the following stressors. You can also go to www.IGiveMyselfPermission.com/downloads to download a copy. Next to each item, put a number from 1 to 10 to describe how intense each is for you. For items you rank at a level 6 or above, take some time to describe what about that item creates stress for you.

_____ Covid-19, RSV, flu

_____ Wars

_____ Gun violence

_____ Political tensions

_____ Injustice (for example, racism, sexism, homophobia, and so on)

_____ Work, work, work (What is work balance?)

_____ Money (making more, not having enough, savings, debt)

_____ Economy (changes in the market, inflation, retirement)

_____ Anger (not getting enough in return, being disrespected)

_____ Guilt (mistakes from the past)

_____ Grief (loss of people)

_____ Grief (loss of a job or autonomy)

_____ Stress/anxiety (fear of the unknown, worrying, overthinking)

_____ Caring for family (parents, children, relatives)

_____ Navigating friendships (old and new friends)

_____ Trauma (pain from past, physical, sexual, racial)

_____ Sicknesses (illnesses, hospitalizations, family members)

_____ Isolation and loneliness (feeling alone, having little time with peers, friends, and family)

_____ Managing relationships (romantic connections, dating, date nights with a partner)

_____ Impact of the environment (allergies, seasonal affective disorder, hurricanes, and so on)

_____ Finding time for fun and travel (seeing the world, having adventures, creating memories)

_____ Negative self-talk

_____ Loss of opportunity (loss of job, business deal gone bad, rejected/rescinded school application)

_____ Balancing religious, civic, and/or community responsibilities

_____ Having hobbies and time for hobbies

After looking at the list, you might say that everything is a stressor. That might be true, and certainly, with one or all of these stressors, it can be difficult to give yourself permission. You may think, *I'm too stressed* or *There's too much to do.* Pay attention to what you tell yourself, and we'll work with these thoughts as you continue reading. Building awareness of the narrative you tell yourself about the social stressors in your life is the key to unlocking your permission.

Barrier #2: Leadership Stress

What does it mean to be a leader? We often attribute the word "leader" to the CEO, C-Suite, captain of the team, or even the most vocal person in the room. But being a leader is more than a title or job, or how much we speak up. Many of us are leaders in our immediate and extended families, the community, places of faith, town or city, sports, or at work. We can be leaders in roles such as manager, team lead, supervisor, and owner, and even as someone working their way up.

When we consistently show up as a leader, there are unique stressors. In *Resonant Leadership*, authors Richard Boyatzis and Annie McKee (2005) call it "power stress." They say that leaders often face unprecedented challenges that can result in a vicious cycle of stress, pressure, sacrifice, and dissonance. When this cycle continues, it can create an experience called *sacrifice syndrome*, where leaders sacrifice too much for too long and reap too little, causing them to feel trapped.

Sacrifice syndrome and the stress that leaders experience interrupt their ability to give themselves permission. Business leaders in particular become hyperfocused on the work, tasks, productivity, profit margins, KPIs (key performance indicators), putting out fires, meeting deliverables, and winning—besides home and family obligations. Giving themselves permission to do something for themselves can fall right off their to-do list. The pressure to lead and be successful can get in the way of going on vacations, resting, and spending quality time with loved ones.

Often, business leaders push these things aside, saying they will get in the way of their work. The authors of *Resonant Leadership* suggest that leaders lack renewal, and therefore, struggle to escape the sacrifice syndrome. Too many leaders believe that giving themselves permission for renewal will take away from productivity and tasks, when renewing and recharging actually helps with their overall goal.

So don't let your definition of leadership keep you trapped in the sacrifice syndrome. Give yourself permission to practice renewal and integrate wellness and time with family and friends into your leadership.

Barrier #3: Injustice Stress

In his 1963 letter from a jail in Birmingham, Alabama, Dr. Martin Luther King Jr. wrote, "Injustice anywhere is a threat to justice everywhere. We are caught in an inescapable network of mutuality, tied in a single garment of destiny. Whatever affects one directly, affects all indirectly."

Injustice is also a threat to giving yourself permission. The pain of experiencing injustices such as sexism, racism, homophobia, ageism, and trauma can produce many negative mental, emotional, and physical issues. When you experience and witness injustice, it can make you second-guess yourself, stop believing in yourself, and think that something is wrong with you. Its internal noise is loud and confusing. You might become overwhelmed by negative self-talk that tells you that you aren't smart, capable, attractive, or deserving of good things.

Giving yourself permission to live boldly, start a new business, go to therapy, take risks, or heal from your trauma can become very difficult after experiencing injustice. If you've never experienced it, you might assume I'm exaggerating. But after almost twenty-five years of listening to people tell me their experiences of injustice, I know its effects are real and not an excuse.

If you advocate and fight for those who have experienced injustice, it can be hard to give yourself permission as well. Often, there's a strong feeling that if you take a break or spend more time with your family, you will fail the people you are trying to help.

Let's look at a definition of one form of injustice: racial trauma.

"Racial trauma is the emotional and physical symptoms often experienced by Black families and people of color due to the everyday experiences of racism and microaggressions. It includes intergenerational injuries resulting from personal and collective experiences of racism" (James 2020). It can include but is not limited to these symptoms: hypervigilance, body aches, shame, fear, insomnia, guilt, headaches, confusion, numbness, anger, lack of productivity, depression, anxiety, lack of desire, and being silent (James 2020).

Other forms of injustice have a similar impact, and with all of these symptoms from injustice, giving yourself permission to speak up for yourself, heal from the toxicity, or take a day off from the fight might be at the bottom of your list, if it's there at all. The injustice wants to steal your joy and purpose. It wants to deprive you of living boldly, finding a job where you are celebrated for your talents, going to therapy, spending quality time with loved ones, or being your full self.

It will not be easy, but you can regain your ability to give yourself permission after the pain of injustice. It will mean admitting you are experiencing it, facing the internal challenges that result from it, and advocating to end the injustice, while also taking care of yourself.

Barrier #4: Family-of-Origin Stress

The last barrier to giving ourselves permission comes from our family—specifically, our family of origin. In the mental health world, our families receive a lot of blame for the internal challenges we face in our lives. The reason behind this blame is the fact that our family, especially our parents, shape our early development, including attachment, character, parts of our personality, behaviors, and beliefs. This shaping happens whether we have two caregivers, one, or none.

Our experiences growing up build our confidence, drive, ambition, sensitivities, insecurities, and empathy, and many other qualities. Our family of origin starts our character development process, and we continue the evolution with our choices in life. The same is true with giving ourselves permission. We first learn how to give ourselves permission by watching our family members. In the areas where they give themselves permission, it becomes easier for us to do the same. For instance, if one or both of our parents give themselves permission to go back to school for a degree later in life, it will help us focus on education.

As I mentioned earlier, I saw my mother work very hard while offering care to everyone else. Similarly, I saw my father work multiple jobs throughout his life and attempt to start several businesses. Through watching their examples, I learned to value hard work. At the same time, I didn't see my mother rest, travel, exercise, or practice self-care. I had to be intentional in my life in giving myself permission in these areas. Some were more challenging than others because of what I learned growing up.

Of course, all the responsibility doesn't belong to our family, but looking at our early experiences can highlight why we have difficulty giving ourselves permission in specific areas. In looking back, ask yourself where you saw your parents or caregivers give themselves permission. What did you learn from your family about work, rest, exercise, food, self-care, money, purpose, education, love, and more?

Reflect on your family of origin and write down your thoughts in a journal. This process can help you realize how you started your narrative about yourself and what you believe you can or can't do. Then you can start the work of changing the narrative.

No matter what you didn't learn as a child, you can start the process of giving yourself permission now. As you read this book, if you find yourself getting stuck, think about which barrier is related to why you are stuck. If you still find yourself stuck after you finish this book, come back and read this section again. It will help you work on your plan to give yourself permission.

You can do this no matter how many barriers are in the way!

Wrapping Up

At the end of every chapter, you will find chapter questions, exercises, and/or reflections. Use these prompts as guides to help explore giving yourself permission. Journaling about these will give you

additional insight into your personal and professional goals. Take
your time to think, feel, and respond to each prompt. Take a break if
you feel overwhelmed and come back to the writing later. You could
also reflect on these questions in quiet time, meditation, or prayer, or
discuss them with a therapist, coach, or trusted friend.

- How does your belief that giving yourself permission is a
  privilege impact you and your choices?

- Which one of the four barriers is the most challenging
  for you? Write down the reasons why this is the most
  challenging area for you.

- What is one thing you learned from your family that
  makes it difficult for you to give yourself permission?

Chapter 2

I Give Myself Permission to Risk, Fail, and Live Boldly

When we give ourselves permission to fail, we, at the same time, give ourselves permission to excel.

—Eloise Ristad

Diego was in his mid-twenties when we first started working together. He was at his first job after college, a job that involved long hours, cold calls, and sales pitches, all while working for a difficult manager. He hated every minute of it but felt he had to pay his dues and show up. He decided to start therapy because he was experiencing a lot of anxiety from the job while at the same time grieving the loss of his father.

Losing a parent at any age can be extremely difficult, but it's especially challenging in your twenties. During this phase of life, it is common to believe that one's parents will be around for the years to come, to guide you through life's ups and downs. A parent's death at this time brings not only loss but also an internal struggle with the concept of mortality. What made Diego's loss even more troubling was that his father had died of a hereditary disease that Diego and his siblings had a significant chance of developing. In a worst-case scenario, it could mean that he would develop this illness before he was forty, which would create a substantial impact on his quality of life, and maybe even early death.

Diego couldn't stop thinking about the future, which meant he couldn't stop thinking about the possibility of dying. Between the pressure of his job and his constant thoughts about his future, he was in the deep end of the pool of anxiety.

We worked on strategies such as breathing exercises, finding ways to stay in the present, and paying attention to his thoughts and the story he was creating. As he processed his grief, we discussed ways he could honor his father.

Diego shared that his father loved to laugh, travel, and live life to the fullest. Thinking about his dad in this way inspired him, but he would quickly come back to feeling like he couldn't be like his dad. He felt trapped by both the job and his anxiety.

Over time, we continued to talk about his self-imposed limitations. Ultimately, he decided to give himself permission to travel, and not just a trip to the beach or to the Caribbean. He wanted to literally see the world. He found creative ways to finance his trips, like taking odd jobs, getting financial support from family members, and couch-surfing along the way.

We stayed in touch during his different stops through email and a travel website he started. Seeing the world opened his eyes to endless possibilities. Giving himself permission to travel led to giving himself permission to take risks while traveling, which expanded to giving himself permission to believe in himself and his future.

When he returned, he knew that one day he could be a CEO, lead his own company, and earn enough money to support advancements to find a cure for his father's disease. He discovered that he had options beyond the job he had been working at just six short months prior to this experience.

Before long, Diego took a leap and started his own business—all because he had worked through his beliefs about his limitations and given himself permission to take risks and live boldly.

Taking Risks

We've heard stories of people who used their last dollar to start their business or made a career change to a different industry, went back to school while working and raising children, moved to a new city on their own, publicly shared their mental health challenges, or defied the odds to experience a high level of success. What's the common theme? They were all willing to take a risk and believe that their dream could happen for them.

It isn't easy to give yourself permission to take risks. Remember those stories in our heads that we discussed earlier? They become louder when we think about taking risks. Our limiting stories about ourselves cause us to question our desires or tell us we'll fail. But you *can* be the person to do that fantastic thing, whatever it is. And it starts with giving yourself permission to take the risk.

In the 2024 Paris Olympics, American track and field star Noah Lyles won a gold medal in the 100-meter race in an amazing photo finish. What was more amazing was the August 4, 2024 statement he shared on X (formerly Twitter) after winning his race. He said, "I have asthma, allergies, dyslexia, ADD, anxiety, and depression. But I will tell you that what you have does not define what you can become. Why Not You!"

He didn't let the narrative about any of his diagnoses stop him from taking a risk and betting on himself. He was willing to give himself permission to risk failing. He believed that amazing things could happen for him, just like they can happen for you. He also used his support systems. Before his gold medal–winning race, he spoke to his therapist, who helped him focus.

What support do you have in place to help you? What risks are you taking? Noah's story is a great reminder for us all to give ourselves permission to take risks and believe in ourselves. Why not you?

Flight-Fight-Freeze Responses

As soon as we get the courage to give ourselves permission to take a risk, we really feel our fears, especially the fear of failing. What if we take the risk and fail? What if [think of your worst-case scenario] happens?

The fear of failing can create multiple reactions. Typically, we hear about fight-or-flight responses when we face challenging or traumatic situations. Sometimes, to avoid risk, we fight against our desires, and at other times, we experience flight, running from the situation or avoiding it in order to avoid the risk.

In the fight mode, the body starts to prepare physically for a perceived threat. But what happens when that perceived threat is failure? When you start to see your desires and goals as threats, you—your mind, body, and emotions—prepare for a fight, but it's a fight against yourself. Ron, whom you read about in the introduction, often found himself in fight mode. As soon as he would share his desire to be a writer, he would go into fight mode and give his desire a counterpunch by quickly saying to himself, *No one will read what I write, so why should I even try?*

In the flight mode, your body prepares to run away or avoid a perceived threat. How do we run away or avoid our desires and goals? We can do this in many ways; one way is to stay busy. Many people will look at someone who is busy and think they are moving toward their goals, but sometimes being busy can be a way to avoid your goals. Being busy can be a choice or a necessity, but either way, it can keep you from your desires. My mother, Gwendolyn, was often busy. This was mainly out of necessity. She had to work long hours at her job, at home, at the church, and for the community, leaving her little time to go back to school or to travel, two desires that were high on her list.

One of the other responses that isn't discussed as often is freezing. Fear has an ability to make us feel stuck, influencing us to do everything but the thing we are afraid of. In the freeze mode, the body is stuck between fight and flight. Instead of preparing to physically engage or run away, the body slows down its responses and everything comes to a halt.

How do you achieve your desires if you are frozen? Many of us freeze more than we realize. We become stuck in our thoughts, actions, and emotions, delaying or completely stopping our ability to move forward. Earlier in this chapter, you read about Diego, who found himself stuck between his job, grief, and desires for the future. He didn't know what to do or how to do it, and it was hard for him to give himself permission to do something different.

Our fears can take up a lot of mental real estate and create a false narrative about who we are and what we're capable of doing. Many of us have multiple desires, goals, and aspirations on our list that we don't pursue because of these fears. During his Naismith

National Basketball Association (NBA) Hall of Fame Speech in 2009, Michael Jordan, six-time NBA champion, said, "Never say never. Because limits, like fears, are often just an illusion."

Is your fear of failing getting in your way? Giving yourself permission to fail means you accept the possibility that you might not succeed; you embrace your fears and find ways to still move forward with your goals, dreams, and aspirations.

Live Boldly

What we're told by those around us and the stories we grow up believing about ourselves can cause us to place limitations on what we think is possible for us. These limitations may be based on race, perceived class, gender, age, sexual identity, and abilities, but they may also be based on the traumas and challenging life events we've experienced.

There is an interesting psychological phenomenon called *learned helplessness*, which often happens when someone experiences many negative situations, causing them to create an internal story that they are powerless to change their situation.

So, when opportunities arise that could help them change their circumstances, they don't take advantage of them. While other people in their lives might see their potential and their limitless possibilities, all they can see are their limitations.

The hardest part about learned helplessness is that when you are in the situation, you don't realize that you're seeing limitations that might not actually be there. You see obstacles and believe that your idea for a business, your desire to start a new relationship, or your hope to break a habit has no chance of success.

As difficult as it might seem, most limitations are mainly in your mind. Yes, there are actual boundaries for some things. For instance, the likelihood of becoming a principal ballet dancer at the American Ballet Theatre without any dance experience, or joining the National

Hockey League for the first time at the age of forty, is slim. But the ability to impact the culture, players, and communities through your ability, effort, creativity, and knowledge is limitless. When you start giving yourself permission to take risks, fail, and live boldly, you take steps closer to your goal. And with each step, you reduce both the actual limitations and the perceived limitations. In *Eleanor* (2020), author David Michaelis presents an account of Eleanor Roosevelt's inspiring life, including stories of the challenges she had to overcome and how she regularly pushed herself to do things outside of her comfort zone. The book includes one of her well-known quotes: "Do one thing every day that scares you."

So today, give yourself permission, and give yourself a chance to live with the kind of boldness that inspires you and others.

Your First Domino

Think about a set of dominoes placed in a formation where each one will hit the next, ending with the last one hitting a lever to reveal a prize. To start this process, you have to hit the first and closest domino. It's the initial step—the catalyst—that starts the entire process. Now, give yourself permission to do *one small thing* that feels doable right now (the first domino), and choose a date for when you will do it.

What will be the first domino that will help you give yourself permission to live with more joy, renewal, or purpose? Will you ask your crush out on a date? Take a class? Pivot to a new career? Decide to be a stay-at-home parent? Sing karaoke at the office party? Learn to swim, ski, play golf, or play an instrument? Devote thirty minutes to yourself (even if it's just to take a nap)? Meet with a coach? Go back to therapy (maybe with a new therapist) after taking a break? Just stop believing that you "can't" or "shouldn't" live more boldly? The initial domino is all you have to think about at this point, not the entire process to get you all the way there.

In the introduction, I shared Ron's story. His first domino was the negative thoughts saying that nothing good would ever happen for him. At the same time, his desire to write and share his perspective never went away. We discussed multiple avenues, from writing a blog to working for a local newspaper to starting a podcast to writing a post on social media. Each time, he felt overwhelmed by the task. As time went on, we discussed recording a podcast episode that he didn't have to publish.

And that's what he did. He recorded two episodes of a podcast. Ron shared that he was nervous, and the negative thoughts made him think the episode wasn't good. To keep himself accountable, he pushed himself further and published the episodes, then shared them with me. I was very proud of Ron because he gave himself permission to try something that had been on his mind for a while. The episodes were good, honest, vulnerable, and funny.

What will your first step be? Who will help you? Who will hold you accountable? Like Ron, you can take the first step and give yourself permission. At www.IGiveMyselfPermission.com/downloads, you'll find a download of this material, and you'll have the opportunity to write down what your first domino will be.

Sometimes, learning more about how other people gave themselves permission can help you to give yourself permission in an area you have been thinking about. Go to www.IGiveMyselfPermission.com/Examples to read and see stories from other people. I also want to hear your stories to share with others. To submit your stories of how you gave yourself permission, please go to www.IGiveMyselfPermission.com/Stories.

Wrapping Up

Let's practice! Take a moment to think about this: imagine you had no limits and no fear of failing, and were willing to take risks. What would you give yourself permission to do? What would bring joy, excitement, adventure, purpose, curiosity, and fun into your life? Write down what comes to mind. Think about what this would look like in your life and note the differences between how your life is now and this ideal version in your mind.

Next, write down what is holding you back. What do you see as your obstacles? What do you tell yourself that prevents you from taking risks, living more boldly, and doing the things you just wrote down? How can you embody a *Why can't I?* and *Why not me?* mindset?

One way to do this is to reflect on your skills, talents, abilities, education, and other parts of you. Remind yourself that you are also capable, just like the people you admire, see on social media, or read about. Pay attention to the negative thoughts that try to tell you it only happens for others and not you. Then pick one area you want to focus on. Do some research, get support from others, develop a plan, and say: *Yes, I can do this. Why not me!*

Chapter 3

I Give Myself Permission to Not Be Perfect

*Our strength lies not in expecting
ourselves to be perfect but in
understanding that our greatest strength
is our ability to learn. Self-compassion
means loving acceptance of current
limitations in a way that supports our
marvelous ability to grow.*

—Dr. Kathryn Ford

"I can never get my mother to acknowledge any of my accomplishments," Alexandra told me during a therapy session. "I try so hard to be perfect, but even that isn't enough for her. Whenever I tell her about something I've achieved, she just starts talking about herself. It's like she's competing with me. When I was a kid, she never even praised me for getting straight As."

Alexandra proceeded to tell me that at thirty-five, her current age, she had risen to the top in her field and was married to the picture-perfect husband with a beautiful child. Yet, she was stressed and unhappy. Trying so hard to always be perfect was taking a toll on her, and her so-called picture-perfect marriage wasn't so perfect after all.

Her husband barely spoke to her, he never helped around the house, and their sex life was nonexistent. Still, she felt she couldn't leave because a divorce would mean she had failed. What would her friends think? What would her mother think?

As a child, Alexandra had developed the unconscious belief that if she could just be perfect, her mother would finally acknowledge her. In therapy, she began to realize that her lifelong desire for perfection was misguided. She was letting her mother's perceptions dictate how she lived her life, yet no matter what she did, her mother simply wasn't capable of giving her the kind of attention she wanted.

We all have a backstory, including Alexandra's mom. Her mother grew up in a time when women's voices and achievements were not acknowledged. She often felt she had to work twice as hard to get the credit she felt she deserved. Throughout the years, she started to make sure other people were aware of all of her hard work. Unfortunately, to this day, she does not recognize the impact this had on her children.

Over the course of our sessions, Alexandra became aware that she had to love herself and stop trying so hard to win the love and acceptance of others. It was her own approval she needed, not her mother's. But that meant giving herself permission to not be perfect.

It meant learning to accept herself as a human being with flaws and struggles. Once she was able to do that, she could also give herself permission to create a life that actually worked for her.

Since then, Alexandra has been able to soften her perfectionist expectations of herself. She has even forgiven her mother for also being imperfect. She didn't go from perfectionism to 100 percent carefree, of course, but that isn't what giving ourselves permission is about. It's about a daily process of recognizing that our desire to be perfect is a sign that we need to receive acceptance from others *and* from ourselves. We have to let perfectionism go as best we can while giving ourselves love and grace. This daily process can bring us to a place of contentment and peace.

Using this daily process, Alexandra learned to catch herself when she pushed toward perfection and to give herself permission to be human. Living her life on her own terms—rather than someone else's imagined terms—opened up a whole new world of possibilities for her. Suddenly she had choices, including getting a divorce. She and her husband were able to split amicably and co-parent better than when they were together. Letting go of perfectionism meant she could give herself permission to do what she truly wanted in every aspect of her life.

The Quest for Perfection

How many of us are like Alexandra without realizing it? We try so hard to "earn" our place in the world, and we're afraid that our success or status will be jeopardized if we make the tiniest mistake. So we strive to get everything just right, while hoping to avoid ever doing anything wrong and ever causing anyone to get mad at us or criticize us. If we can just do that, we won't get into trouble, we won't be discarded, and everyone will accept us. On an unconscious level, we think that if we could just be perfect, we'd be truly loved.

But there's no such thing as perfection. It's an illusion, a fantasy. Not only is it impossible for a human being to ever be perfect, but no two people will agree on what perfection even means.

We've all seen what the quest for perfection can do to people. The ballet dancer who reaches the pinnacle of her profession but hurts her body along the way with cigarettes and struggles with eating disorders. The class valedictorian who dies by suicide because he didn't get into an Ivy League college and saw that as his only chance for success. The parent who pushes their child to be the best at everything (school, sports, and music) because their child's success is a reflection of their parenting. The man who works out constantly because he believes his strength and chiseled abs will help him avoid judgments of his character. The woman who has to cook the perfect holiday meal for her mother-in-law. The athlete who feels they must win at all costs because they're a failure without a perfect record. Or someone like Alexandra, who stays too long in a miserable marriage because she can't bear the thought of being seen as imperfect.

Sometimes we don't even give ourselves permission to acknowledge that we did a good job if it wasn't the "perfect" job as we've defined it. We don't acknowledge our own accomplishments any more than Alexandra's mother acknowledged her daughter's.

We might think that perfectionism is a good thing in school or in the workplace, but studies have shown that perfectionists don't perform better than nonperfectionists at work. The authors of a 2018 *Harvard Business Review* article evaluated ninety-five studies on perfectionism conducted over four decades, which included almost 25,000 people of working age. They found that perfectionists are also more prone to stress, burnout, anxiety, and depression (Swider et al. 2018).

At the same time, another study of more than 40,000 students in the US, Canada, and Britain found that perfectionism rose 33 percent between 1989 and 2016 (Curran and Hill 2019). According to the Centers for Disease Control (CDC), suicide is now the second leading cause of death in the US in young people from ages ten to fourteen and twenty-five to thirty-four, and the third leading cause of death for those ages fifteen to twenty-four (2022). Clearly, perfectionism is a rampant problem.

The Root Cause of Perfectionism

Perfectionism is rooted in insecurity. Most people succumb to it because they're afraid they aren't good enough unless they're perfect. Perfectionists are afraid to show any vulnerability or admit flaws because, in their mind, that means they aren't worthy. But no one is without chinks in their armor. The key to healing perfectionism is not just relaxing our expectations but also dealing with our insecurities. We must learn to give ourselves a break and relinquish our unreasonable requirements, like Alexandra started to do.

Of course, when I advise that you surrender the need to be perfect, I'm not saying you should never strive for excellence. With excellence, we're doing our best. With perfectionism, even excellence isn't good enough because we're trying to reach some impossible superhuman ideal.

When I have a speaking engagement or a media appearance, for example, I don't worry if I fumble over my words a little bit here and there. People like it when we show our imperfections. It makes us relatable. I'm someone on their television screen, but I'm still human. Of course, it took me some time to feel comfortable allowing myself to fumble. I used to think I had to be perfect when I appeared on television. I had to give myself permission to be human over and over.

As we saw with Alexandra, she was afraid of never receiving her mother's approval, which made her feel insecure. At the same time, she realized that her mother had been hurt in the past and was seeking her own acceptance through competition. Everything changed once Alexandra became aware of the cause of her own perfectionism and viewed her mother's full story through a more realistic adult lens. Only then did she accept that her mother's pain would probably always stand in the way of the approval and love she'd always hoped for. This awareness allowed her to let go of the need for her mother's approval and give it to herself instead.

Of course, softening your expectations and insecurities isn't as easy as just saying you will. Perfectionism becomes a deeply ingrained habit, and it always takes time to change habitual behavior. The first step is just to become aware of your perfectionism and the fears you hold about not being good enough. Once you're conscious of your tendency to put this undue pressure on yourself, you can start to pay mindful attention every day. Then, like Alexandra, you can begin to catch yourself when you start to push too hard. You can consciously take a deep breath and say to yourself, *I don't have to be perfect today. I'm going to let myself be human and know that I'm acceptable as an imperfect human being.* You get to decide exactly how much you want to strive toward your goal, while also offering yourself the kindness you deserve.

As you build more and more experience, you'll begin to recognize your negative self-talk in the moment instead of afterward. The more this happens, you'll gradually reduce the negative self-talk to nothing, and then replace the nothing with positive self-talk. This process allows you to make a different choice.

Over time, the act of changing negative self-talk to positive will become a habit. Gradually, you'll soften your previous perfectionist tendencies until you make decisions based on what you truly want or need in the moment. You'll relax your expectations and see yourself as acceptable and lovable as you are, shortcomings and all.

It becomes an equation to live by: add self-love and subtract perfectionism. Your self-love will increase as your need for perfection decreases. It's a great way to live, and it opens up all sorts of possibilities for giving yourself permission in your life. Like Alexandra found out, once she no longer had to live up to the excessive expectations she had placed on herself for most of her life, she had countless options to choose from.

Perfection as an Act of Survival

I realize that it's easy to say, "Just stop trying to be so perfect all the time!" But it isn't necessarily easy to do. Let's say you're in a high-profile job that's very competitive. If you don't stay at the top of your game, you'll likely lose your job or your status in your profession. Maybe you're an athlete who can maintain your position only if you push yourself beyond your limits every day in the gym, at practice, or in the game or match. Or you're first chair in the orchestra and you know that if you slip, there's someone waiting to take your position, so you practice over and over again.

It's also a harsh reality that women and people of color often feel they have to work twice as hard just to be considered or even acknowledged. They find that they have to be perfect in order to get a job that might be given easily to an imperfect person of another gender or race. Unfortunately for many generations, perfection was and still can be an act of survival for women, people of color, and many others who have experienced discrimination. They have had to maintain perfect standards to create opportunities for themselves, their family, their community, and others with similar identities.

Sometimes, striving for perfection kept them alive or helped them escape from a harmful situation. The difficult truth is that not everyone has the privilege of releasing perfection as a standard. At the same time, because others accepted the cost in previous generations through movements, revolutions, changes in policy, or living by imposed limitations, many of us can now entertain the thought of living without perfectionism. These previous generations did a lot to empower us to have more choices than they had.

I understand that the need to be perfect is sometimes the result of our current lived experience. Yet constantly pushing ourselves to the brink can take over and impact every aspect of our lives. What will you do with the options you have in front of you, even if they're limited in comparison to the options available to someone with more resources or who is of a different gender or racial background?

Reaching great heights in life is enormously gratifying, but it usually comes at a cost. I've worked with people who pushed themselves hard to get to the top of their field, career, or sport, only to later regret what they lost along the way. You are the only person who can determine if the cost is worth it, but you must take the time to reflect and consider what that cost is.

Often, we keep pushing harder because we think we're supposed to. Unfortunately, if this behavior goes on long enough, it can reach levels of burnout that affect our health, both physical and mental. When people are in a state of burnout for too long, they can sometimes sabotage the career, sport, family, or organization they worked so hard for.

The most important question is: are you fulfilled? If your fulfillment in your job, home, community, relationship, or position far outweighs the stress and pressure of striving so hard, that's what matters. If, on the other hand, you're secretly miserable but feel stuck because you've spent so many years getting to the pinnacle, it may be time to rethink what matters most in your life.

Far too many people spend years and tens of thousands of dollars on education, training in a sport, practicing their musical instrument, or something else to get to a perfect place—only to discover that they hate what they expected to love. They feel trapped. How can they possibly pursue a different path after they've invested so much? They may believe they don't have any options, and it could be true that their options are limited if perfection has been their only path for so long.

But even if it takes time, they're entitled to give themselves permission to try something new. There will never be an alternate way of living if they simply give up and assume perfection is the only option, even though it hasn't worked for them. That's what Alexandra did for a long time. She couldn't see a way out of her marriage, but the only thing truly in her way was her own thinking and limited beliefs.

My mother believed she had to be the perfect parent and work nonstop. She always wanted to travel, but she never gave herself permission because she couldn't see it as a possibility. She might never have been able to take a luxury vacation, but she and my father surely could have found a way to take a trip now and then.

Giving yourself permission will help you make the next step. Both big and small changes might prove painful in the short run, but if you stay in a situation that makes you unhappy all the time, you opt for long-term nonstop pain. Life is simply too short to live like that. The short-term pain is worth it for the long-term gain.

The Importance of Balance

In all of these circumstances, balance is key. Just like perfection, balance is an ideal we will never quite reach. Unlike perfection, however, striving for balance is healthy, even when we don't quite get there. The more we can achieve it in every area of our life, the better we'll feel.

When we don't give ourselves permission to be imperfect, we almost always don't give ourselves permission in other areas either—to play and rest, to love and be loved, to let go and move on, to be authentic, or to take good care of ourselves. And a well-balanced life includes all of these things: work, love, family, friends, play, and recreation. A perfectionist attitude doesn't allow for most of these important aspects of living. Clearly it isn't so perfect after all!

That's why without balance, we sacrifice our physical, mental, and spiritual health. I admire four-time Olympic gold medalist Simone Biles a great deal for the decision she made to pull out of the Olympics in 2021. She had been expected to win at least three more gold medals, but the pressure got so bad that she found herself with an episode of the "twisties" (when a gymnast can't orient themselves in the air and no longer knows which way is up or down). When she got lost in the air during a vault, she realized just how dangerous her situation had become. Rather than push herself to the point that she could have lost everything, Simone opted for balance. She gave herself permission to do what was best for her and her well-being.

Though she took heat from some people for her decision, she had the courage to put her mental health before her quest for perfection. She's a true champion for all she has done for gymnastics and so many across the world. If she stopped there, she would still be the GOAT, the greatest of all time. But after taking care of herself, she returned to competition and to the Olympics to add to her medal count. It was an amazing example of giving yourself permission, if you ask me. She stopped something that was harmful, took care of herself, and then went back to competing at the highest stage in the world.

Then there are the young women who go to extraordinary lengths to look thin and beautiful as they try to live up to the images of the models they see online, in magazines, and now in artificial intelligence–generated images. But even the models can't live up to these unrealistic expectations, so the images must be edited, filtered, airbrushed, and more to remove every supposed tiny imperfection. The women who see these ads are trying to live up to an image that's 100 percent impossible. It's startling how brutal we can be to ourselves and each other when we apply perfectionist standards.

When we're focused on trying to be perfect, it's impossible to get anywhere near balance. We inevitably identify our self-worth with our perfectionist persona. When we don't meet those standards or expectations, we might feel depressed or even contemplate suicide because we believe our life is over if we're imperfect.

But nothing could be further from the truth. Giving ourselves permission to be imperfect is exactly when our real life begins—real as in human and balanced. When we lose something, we automatically assume the alternative will be worse, but it just might be the best thing that ever happened to us. Sometimes we have no idea what wonderful experiences are in store for us when we don't get what we thought we wanted.

If we maintain a balanced point of view and remove the blinders that our perfectionism puts over our eyes, we can see that there are many ways for everyone to be happy. Give yourself permission to be human, not perfect; to be happy, not trapped; and to be the best version of you rather than some superhuman ideal.

Wrapping Up

Try the following exercise to determine if a perfectionist attitude is standing in your way. The questions can help you unearth what you're truly feeling; only then will you be able to give yourself permission to not be perfect and open yourself up to more possibilities.

You can download this exercise at www.IGiveMyselfPermission. com/downloads, or if you prefer, you can write your answers to these questions in a journal. Take time to answer each one thoughtfully and dig deep to discover underlying feelings. It's important to keep your answers so that you can refer to them later. This is how you gain new insights about where in your life you aren't giving yourself the permission you could. As always, if you find yourself stuck or very distressed by the questions, please seek the help of a professional coach or therapist.

- In what, if any, areas of your life do you feel pressured? Do you feel you have to be the best to be accepted? These are probably the areas where you are imposing perfectionism on yourself.

- Choose the area in which you feel the most pressure. What do you fear would happen if you granted yourself permission to be human? If it has to do with your job, sport, community engagement, or home life, do you fear you would lose this part of your life?

- If you want to leave a situation in which you feel pressured to be perfect and you have the means/opportunity to leave, what's preventing you from giving yourself that permission? Do you worry that others will judge you? If they do, will the consequences truly be as awful as you imagine, or will it just be temporarily unpleasant? Do you hold the opinions of those who might judge you as more important than your own? If you do, it's time to correct that misconception. Your opinion is the one that matters most!

- Are you living your life on your own terms, or are you living based on what you believe others expect of you? Are you living based on what you believe you "should" do? Where did this belief about what you should do originate from, and does it have anything to do with what you really want?

- Do you give others permission to be less than perfect, or do you expect the same perfection of them as you expect of yourself? Some of us grant grace to others but not to ourselves. Others of us have excessive expectations of everyone. Stop and think about the expectations you have for yourself and for others. Are they reasonable and sustainable, or do they put undue pressure on anyone who must meet those expectations?

- Can you imagine relaxing your standards a bit? How would that feel, and what fears would it bring to the surface? Do you feel like you will let a client or patient down, lose an important case, miss a valued opportunity with family, ministry, or advocating for an underserved or misrepresented group because you aren't as perfect as you could be?

- Would the world fall apart if you weren't perfect? Do you fear that you'd find out you aren't indispensable if, for example, you took a two-week vacation and discovered that your office operated just fine without you? Take a moment to truly imagine what might happen if you dropped the ball. Would it be as catastrophic as you think? Could you, for example, ask your boss to let you leave on time a couple of nights per week rather than work three hours of overtime every night?

- If you didn't feel the pressure to be perfect, what would you give yourself permission to do? (Take plenty of time to answer this one!)

- Where can you begin to soften your striving and offer yourself the self-love that comes from accepting your humanness?

- Does your fear of not being perfect keep you from an opportunity for growth? For example, if you aren't able to perfectly prepare a healthy meal every night for your family like that mom you follow on social media, instead of feeling like you're inadequate, can you find ways to take the pressure off? Could you incorporate your family in meal preparation, develop cooking days, or use a meal service to assist you? This change would allow others to grow and allow you to learn to accept help.

Chapter 4

I Give Myself Permission to Love and Be Loved

Being deeply loved by someone gives you strength, while loving someone deeply gives you courage.

—Lao Tzu

When their relationship hit a crisis, Adelle and her husband started therapy. Divorce had come up multiple times, but they were trying to hold on for the kids. They were hoping to give their relationship one last try after years of challenges, from finances and household chores to intimacy issues.

After multiple intense sessions where they were unable to see each other's perspective or be vulnerable with each other, they decided to get a divorce. Sometime afterward, Adelle reached out to work with me individually. She wasn't sure if she wanted to get married again, but she knew she wanted companionship. The idea of dating both excited and terrified her.

"It's been a long time since I dated, flirted, or hooked up with someone other than my ex," Adelle told me. "It's been a total of thirty years that included three years of dating, twenty-five years of marriage, and two years since the divorce. I have no idea what I'm doing."

We talked about dating now versus thirty years ago. She had met her ex in college during their senior year. Finding time for each other felt easy. But now? She had work, co-parenting the (now adult) kids, and other obligations. It was hard to find time for herself, much less dating. On top of that, she knew nothing about dating apps.

"Honestly, the dating apps feel overwhelming," she admitted, "and I feel like I'm too old to date on a screen." Colleagues and her kids had talked about the apps, but Adelle was skeptical. As we went deeper into her reticence, however, we discovered that her worries went far beyond just dating apps.

Eventually, she became aware that she struggled with self-love. She felt she wasn't worthy of love and that she was unattractive at her age. She would often do things for others, but because her self-love was lacking, it was hard for her to ask for what she wanted and needed for herself. "I'm not even sure if I have any love left in the tank after the divorce," she told me.

Many times, during her marriage, she thought, *If I get divorced, I don't know if I'll ever get married again. It's so draining.* As a child, Adelle got conflicting messages about relationships. Several of the women in her family were single after difficult experiences, and several of the men in her family were on their second or third marriages. Adelle struggled to give herself permission to love again after the pain of her family history and the disappointment of her own marriage. At the same time, she struggled to give herself permission to be loved and to believe she was lovable.

Adelle is far from alone in these struggles. They're an immensely common problem. So, in this chapter, we'll talk about giving yourself permission to love and be loved, and how that permission can impact your life.

Love Is a Vulnerable Act

Love can be rewarding and scary at the same time. When you love someone—such as a romantic partner, friend, or family member—and they hurt you or the connection ends, it can be hard to love again. The pain of being heartbroken sometimes makes us want to avoid getting close to anyone.

Some of us are "love hopefuls." We keep trying to rebuild friendships, relationships, or family connections. One challenge to being a love hopeful is that we might not see ourselves as deserving of love in return. We might find it easy to care for others and make sacrifices for them, but like Adelle, it might be harder for us to ask for what we need for ourselves. This usually happens because of the narratives about love that we witnessed and experienced in our past. Adelle was ready to start dating again, but the real work was for her to trust that she was lovable.

In an ideal state, love is bidirectional, going both ways between you and the other person. Most of the time, we believe that we should give love, but true love includes receiving love as well.

Receiving has two dimensions. First, the other person has to participate in the love exchange and offer us that love. The complete exchange includes giving and receiving love while being vulnerable enough to ask for what we want and need from the other person.

The second dimension to receiving love is being willing to accept what the other person offers. We are sometimes not receptive to love because we feel we don't deserve it or we believe we should only give. When this is the case, it's important to give yourself permission to be loved.

Adelle thought that she couldn't compete with other single women because of how she saw herself. Deep down, she felt that she was flawed, and that's why her marriage didn't work out. For most of her life, she thought she wasn't good enough and that if she just gave more or loved more, she could earn the love of others. But then it all came crashing down.

If we don't give ourselves permission to be loved, it's impossible for someone to truly give us the love we need. Maintaining a negative self-image and narrative blocks our ability to receive love. Giving ourselves permission to be loved involves believing that we're lovable regardless of our faults and mistakes. We have to learn to believe that someone will be willing to care for us, think about us, consider us, touch us, and make sacrifices for us because we're worthy of that love.

Givers and Takers

Relationships (romantic, friendships, and family connections) can teach us a lot about ourselves and about life. When I was in college, it felt like I was learning the same lesson from multiple directions. Through my friendships and dating life, I realized that some people are givers and some are takers.

Givers tend to find it easy to give love and focus on others, but they might not be vulnerable with their emotions and can struggle with receiving love. Takers tend to find it easy to receive love and focus on their own wants and needs, but even though they might be vulnerable with their own emotions, they struggle with giving love.

Like anything in life, the extremes of both givers and takers can create a negative experience. An extreme giver is used to putting others before themselves, maybe even to the point of becoming a martyr. They may like to control the emotional aspect of the interaction so that they're hardly ever vulnerable, but that makes it difficult for others to connect with them emotionally. This difficulty can deprive the relationship of trust and emotional safety.

An extreme taker is used to putting themselves before others, maybe even to the point where it creates active harm in their relationships. They might use manipulative actions to get what they want at the expense of the other person, which can make it difficult for them to understand what the other person is feeling. This dynamic also deprives the relationship of trust and emotional safety.

While in college, I still had my rose-colored glasses on, and I believed that most people were givers. I knew that there were bad actors in the world, and I experienced my fair share of them. But I still maintained an optimistic view about most people.

After some disappointing and heartbreaking interactions, I started to see a pattern. My family often quoted a biblical verse that says, in essence, *to whom much is given, much is required.* The translation in my mind was that I should give my all to others without the hope that they would reciprocate. What I didn't fully grasp at that point was that some people were learning a different message: that they should ask for what they wanted and needed without giving anything in return.

These lessons about givers and takers allowed me to give myself permission to build my meaningful connections with people who were willing to give love to me while receiving my love as well.

Giving yourself permission to love and be loved means choosing relationship partners well. If you are primarily a giver, are you giving yourself permission to also receive love? If you are primarily a taker, are you giving yourself permission to give love to others? If you are a giver, and most of the people in your life are takers, you will reinforce that pattern until you ask for what you want and work on believing that you deserve love. This imbalance happens because we are so busy giving love that we fail to show our vulnerability by sharing our needs. Therefore, we keep the flow of love in one direction and reestablish that our role is to love the other person instead of simultaneously being loved ourselves.

On the other hand, if you are a taker, and most of the people in your life are givers, it could reinforce that pattern unless you ask other people what they want and need. One thought that can be helpful is to recognize that other people deserve love. Sometimes takers can seem as if they are not thinking about the needs of other people. This lack of care for others can happen because we are busy asking for what we want and trying to find ways to receive it without focusing on what the other person needs. Here again, we keep the flow of love in one direction and reestablish that our role is to be loved by others instead of simultaneously loving them as well.

I have realized over time that we all have the capacity to be both the giver and the taker. For most of us, there are places where people see us as a giver and other places where people see us as a taker. Then there are relationships where the giving and receiving is reciprocal and evens out.

I have learned to surround myself with people who are capable of giving and receiving in relationships, at least in a way that's balanced over time. I have also learned to limit the number of people in my life who are takers because I have a limited amount I can give. I have sought mentors and advisors who can be a source of information and wisdom, and in those situations, I'm the receiver. Still, they have said that I give to them because I'm willing to apply their advice, and they receive from me when they witness my success. Of course, the opposite is true in situations where I'm the advisor or mentor.

For me, the balance looks like this:

- People I mainly give to   20%

- Mutually beneficial relationships   60%

- People I mainly receive from   20%

Estimate as best you can the percentages of people in your life who fit each category. Do you have many mutually beneficial giving and receiving relationships? If not, you will want to work toward increasing that percentage.

Permission to Be Intimate

Giving yourself permission to love and be loved includes giving yourself permission to experience all levels of intimacy, both nonsexual and sexual. Depending on your life experiences (and some would say depending on your gender), when you hear the word "intimacy," only one of those definitions may come to mind.

A couple I worked with told me that ten years had passed since they'd had sex. Even though this was a significant loss for them, they wanted to work on their connection with each other. They had spent many years working and taking care of their children (who were adults at the time I worked with this couple). They were retired and had some medical issues between them that also impacted their ability to have sex. With the loss of sexual intimacy, they didn't want to lose their nonsexual connection.

Throughout our sessions, they worked on being more vulnerable with each other and sharing what they wanted and needed from the relationship. They started going on date nights, which included telling their adult children they were unavailable once a week. (Even though their children were adults, they often came over and were always in need of something.) This couple went from thinking about divorce to rejuvenating their bond and mutual love. They would hold hands, cuddle on the couch, and rotate planning date night. Their sexual relationship didn't change, but they were able to give themselves permission to love and be loved by working on their non-sexual intimacy.

Permission to love and be loved includes being vulnerable enough with your partner to receive the love you want and need. This includes how you want to spend time, how you want to be touched, what turns you on, what brings you pleasure, what makes you feel safe, what's fun to you, and much more.

It's important that you also give yourself permission to give and receive pleasure. This means naming and describing what that looks like for you. Your partner can't know unless you verbalize it. Giving yourself permission to love and be loved includes talking about con-nection, intimacy, pleasure, and vulnerability.

There are a few things you can do to give yourself permission to love and be loved:

- Think about if it's easier for you to give love to others or to receive love from others.

    - If you are a taker, create room for other people and give yourself permission to love others.

    - If you are a giver, work on being more vulnerable and asking for the love you need from others.

- Think about how love and intimacy are connected for you.

- Practice being vulnerable with your partner and explore both sexual and nonsexual intimacy.

- Practice giving yourself permission to give and receive pleasure while you give yourself permission to love and be loved.

Giving and receiving love both require internal work, reflection, and permission. If you haven't started the journey to loving and being loved, take a chance and try a dating app, or ask your partner to tell you ways you can love them. Share something with your friend that you need from the friendship, or perhaps tell a family member you want to spend more quality time with them. Finally, practice writing and/or saying this daily: *Love is for everyone, including me. I can give love and receive love. I don't have to choose.*

Wrapping Up

Loving others and being loved by others shape our daily experiences. Maybe you didn't realize how nervous you are about dating again, or you now realize you have more takers in your life than givers. Perhaps the type of intimacy you want doesn't match what you are receiving. To gain more insights about yourself, take out your journal and answer the following questions. You can also download them at www.IGiveMyselfPermission.com/downloads.

- Love starts with self-love. What are you doing to practice positive self-love? What are you doing that makes you feel good?

- Reflect on how you think about giving and receiving love. What messages did you receive about love? Was the message you received the same for friends, family members, and romantic partners?

- How have those messages and your life experiences shaped your narrative about yourself and love? How has a negative self-image kept you from giving yourself permission to receive love?

- Does it feel easy to give love and make sacrifices for others while not fully asking for your own wants and needs? (If so, you might be a giver.)

- Does it feel easy to receive love from others, to ask for your wants and needs, while not fully giving love in the same way to others? (If so, you might be a taker.)

- List your closest relationships: family, friends, associates, colleagues, and partner. Put them in these categories:

    - People I mainly give to

    - Mutually beneficial relationships

    - People I mainly receive from

- Are your proportions roughly 20 percent, 60 percent, 20 percent? Or is your ratio of giving and receiving love out of balance?

- When you hear the word "intimacy," do you think of one type? If so, which aspect of intimacy do you think about?

Chapter 5

I Give Myself Permission to Let Go and Move On

Sometimes letting things go is an act of far greater power than defending or hanging on.

—Eckhart Tolle

started working with Ty early in my career and was eager to help him solve his problem. Our time together taught me a lot about being a therapist and executive coach.

In a multiyear affair, Ty felt bad that he was hurting his wife but also didn't want to hurt his other partner. He valued his marriage and the years they'd spent together, so at first, I thought he wanted to find a way to end the affair and reconnect with his wife.

But after a few sessions, Ty mentioned that ending the affair felt difficult. Then he started to share challenges in his marriage that made him unhappy. He loved his wife and their friendship, but their sex life was nonexistent. They also didn't spend a lot of quality time together. I started to think that maybe he wanted to end his marriage and continue with his affair. As we progressed, I learned that his wife knew about the affair, and his other partner knew about his wife. Despite this, the affair had gone on for more than a decade. On some level, they had all agreed to stay in this multiperson relationship.

I thought I would acknowledge this fact and ask Ty if he wanted to keep his connection to both women. Surprisingly, he said no, even though that was his reality. He said he wished he could just escape it all. So I offered another option. "Do you want to end the relationships with both women and be by yourself?" I asked. Ty liked the thought of this idea but knew he wouldn't because he didn't want to hurt either person.

He was stuck, and frankly, so was I. It was hard for him to see any option as a viable way forward without feeling discomfort. I thought there was a "right" path for him, but eventually, I realized that he was blocked from making any decision at all because he couldn't give himself permission to let go of either relationship.

In my case, I struggled to give myself permission to see multiple paths for Ty. Making decisions, especially big ones, can be difficult. Staying in our current position, relationship, or mindset might feel more comfortable than giving ourselves permission to let go of it and move on to the next thing. What we know keeps us stuck, even if it isn't working for us, because the unknown makes us more anxious. Of course, in some cases, the unknown is the best option. Giving ourselves permission to let go and move on can be better for us in the long run.

So, in this chapter, we'll talk about a couple of common scenarios in life when we might struggle to let go and move on.

The Other Parent Trap

Many parents struggle to provide their children with the gradual buildup of independence that eventually leads them to leave the house for college, the military, or a job. It can be hard to let our children go even when they are adults. The bond we have with them makes us want to keep them close. Letting them explore the world and become their full selves is scary because we can't be sure of protecting them from danger or costly decisions.

When we give ourselves permission to let our children move on, we have to let them make their own decisions, which might also mean making mistakes. Because we care for them so much, we don't want to see them get hurt or endanger their future. At the same time, if we don't let go, it prevents them from figuring out how to navigate life on their own terms.

Letting go and moving on doesn't mean we don't interact with them as they get older, share our opinion if they request it, and even support them along the way. It just means that we give them space to make their own choices and recover from their mistakes, if necessary. It also means giving ourselves permission to be patient so that we don't jump in to rescue them while they figure it out.

This can make us feel like we're trapped because, while we want to help them, we also have to trust that we've equipped them with the tools and skills they need for their lives and future. If you find yourself having a hard time letting go and giving your adult children space, consider talking to a therapist to help you during this phase of life.

Of course, young adults also have to let go and move on. It's a two-way street. Many young people struggle to make life choices and launch into adulthood. The goal is to have an adult-to-adult relationship with their parents. While they might never be able to give to their parents as much as they receive, an adult-to-adult relationship creates a giver-and-receiver dynamic. To do this, young adults have to take on more responsibility for their life and become comfortable with more autonomy.

Giving themselves permission to let go doesn't mean they have to disregard what their parents and loved ones say, or refuse to receive help when they need it. But it does mean becoming willing to own their path, make choices, know when to ask for help, and learn how to recover from mistakes, no matter how scary.

If you have young-adult children who are struggling to let go and launch into adulthood, consider suggesting they see a therapist to help them move on.

The Habits We Keep

Giving yourself permission to let go and move on can also apply to habits you want to stop. We all have habits, some of which produce results we like and some of which produce results we dislike. Habits might include routines we have in the morning before our day starts, an affirmation we say before a test or a big game, our gym workout before dinner, our sweet treat when we feel overwhelmed, or biting our nails when we're nervous.

Many books have been written about understanding and overcoming habits. *The Power of Habits* (Duhigg 2012) does a great job of helping people understand their triggers or the classic conditioning that reinforces their habits. For instance, biting your nails is the habit, but the trigger is your upcoming exam. Over time, going to class or thinking about the class becomes the trigger, and you automatically start to bite your nails.

Atomic Habits (Clear 2018) is also an excellent book that can help people change or create new habits through habit stacking and starting small. After reading *Atomic Habits*, my wife started to put on her workout clothes before she began her morning routine. This habit-stacking technique made it easier for her to work out before she started her day.

To let go, for example, starting small might mean that in the beginning, you just refrain from biting your nails while you're at home studying until you're able to give it up all the time. Motivational author and speaker James Clear (2018) contends that our willpower gets tired when we try to let go of a habit cold turkey. In my experience, only a small percentage of people have been able to stop an addiction or even a habit cold turkey.

To move on, starting small might involve creating a new positive habit to replace the old negative one. For example, you might want to begin to meditate. Starting small would mean meditating for two to five minutes a day as you build up to twenty minutes and then an hour.

What these books and many others miss about habits, however, are the inner narratives that make us more susceptible to them. In order to truly change a habit, you have to explore the thoughts you have about yourself, your abilities, your family, and the other people in your situation. A negative inner dialogue can fuel habitual behavior, so it's important to uncover these thoughts through reflection, journaling, and/or therapy. Once you've done that, you can work on changing the beliefs and thoughts, as you start small and work on habit stacking. We'll talk more about changing negative inner narratives as you continue reading through the chapters.

Anxiety's Part in Holding On

When I first started my mental health career twenty-plus years ago, the word "anxiety" wasn't widely used in nonclinical conversations. Now, people use it often and are more aware when they feel it. Still, like depression, anxiety is too often a mental health diagnosis that people believe others experience but not themselves.

Thirty-one percent of the US adult population has experienced an anxiety disorder at some point in their lives, according to the National Comorbidity Survey (2001–2003). That said, we all feel anxious at some point, whether before a final exam, a game that could get our team into the playoffs, a final concert in front of a large audience, a speech, a date, an important business meeting, or many other situations. That kind of anxious feeling is normal, and whether we have a normal temporary anxiety or a clinical diagnosis of anxiety, our feelings can prevent us from letting go and moving on.

The anxious feelings try to influence us to hold on when it would be healthier to let go and move on. They might make us believe that a good outcome won't be possible if we let go, so we shouldn't even try. We *catastrophize*, or imagine the worst possible outcome, as our anxiety spirals and we assume our life will be worse than it already is.

Of course, we can't be 100 percent certain that letting go will be better than our current circumstances. But if we're unhappy, we doom ourselves to staying that way unless we're willing to risk change.

This is the very reason why we have to give ourselves permission—because doing so is a declaration or mantra. It's a way of being that confronts the anxiety we feel and helps us see hope and possibility. Eventually, like Ty, we all have to take the leap to move on to the next thing.

Wrapping Up

Your responses to these questions will help you see what prevents you from letting go and moving on. You can respond in your journal or download the questions at www.IGiveMyselfPermission.com/ downloads.

- Evaluate the connections you have in your life (romantic, friendship, family, community, and work). Are any of those relationships stuck or harmful to you? Is it time to move on?

- Are you stuck in a dilemma like Ty, unable to choose between two options? What would you need in order to give yourself permission to make a choice, let go, and move on?

- Does anything get in the way of you moving on from an unhealthy connection? What makes it difficult?

- If you were to move on, what would you be able to do with your time and energy that you can't do now?

- As a parent, are you struggling with letting go of your kids? Is there someone who can support you during this time? Have you shared with your child(ren) that you want to help them become more independent?

- As a young adult, are you struggling with letting go and launching your life with less dependance on your parents? Is there someone who can support you during this time? Have you shared with your parent(s) that you want to do things with less of their help?

- When you think about letting go and moving on, what makes you most anxious? What could go right if you moved on?

- Who could you ask for support to help you move on?

- What negative beliefs and thoughts are influencing your decisions and habits? Are there any areas where adjustments need to be made?

- What is a negative habit that you would like to let go of and move on from? How could you start small or habit-stack it?

- Does your anxiety keep you from letting go? Try reflecting on your anxiety and negative thoughts, journaling about them, meditating, and/or seeking the help of a therapist to ease them.

Chapter 6

I Give Myself Permission to Change Family Scripts

Be proud of the way you chose not to repeat the cycle again.

—Yasmine Cheyenne

I first met Nia when she was a freshman in college. She was the first person in her family to attend college. Her parents had immigrated from Nigeria to become American citizens, and she and her siblings were all born in the United States. Nia was the oldest and often had the responsibility of taking care of her brother and sister, who were five and seven years younger. This included modeling behavior, cooking, and actually watching them while her parents went to work.

Nia's mom worked as a phlebotomist at a hospital, and her father worked as a mechanic for the city's transportation system. Her mother went back to Nigeria once or twice a year to check in with family, and since she was also the oldest of her siblings, many family members looked to her for both emotional and financial support.

Nia's mother regularly sent almost half of every paycheck to her family, which created a financial burden at times. This practice of sending money back to a home country is called remittance (Gibson 2025). While growing up, Nia admired this strong connection to family and the desire to care for them. She would say, "It's what you do and what you are expected to do."

Indirectly, she learned this value by watching her mom's sacrifice. Directly, her mom told her and her siblings that they were all expected to one day contribute to her efforts to build a house in Nigeria.

Both of Nia's parents had high expectations for her and what she could achieve in the future. They believed that coming to the United States would provide their children with the opportunity to become whatever they wanted to be in life, but they had specific thoughts about what careers that would entail. They wanted Nia to become a medical doctor, her brother to become a lawyer, and her sister to become an engineer.

They started to direct Nia toward the medical path in middle school. They put her in programs outside of school, while also strongly suggesting she focus on math and science classes. They believed that being a medical doctor would command a lot of respect in the US and internationally, and that she would make a great salary and be able to help the family both financially and medically. Once Nia was in college, her parents wanted her to major in one of the sciences while following a pre-med track.

At first, Nia thought becoming a doctor would be cool, but that thought changed over time. Although her grades were good and she was ambitious, with a great work ethic, she hated seeing blood. She just wasn't passionate about being a doctor. Instead, she found herself connected to other disciplines, such as business and English.

The truth is that in many countries, cultures, and families, it's normal for parents to prescribe and direct their children to pursue a particular career, marry a certain person, or make other decisions. What Nia's parents were doing wasn't abnormal, and they were doing it with good intentions so that she could have the resources for a great life.

Many families, cultures, and countries operate from a collectivistic perspective, where the expectation is that people work together for the good of the family and/or community. In this model, that could mean sacrificing personal goals for the goals of the many. The South African and Zulu word *Ubuntu*, which means "I am because we are," embodies this perspective.

In contrast to collectivistic cultures, American culture encourages a more individualistic perspective, where the expectation is that people strive for self-actualization, find their individual purpose, and chart their own course. They can use their success to help and support others, but they're expected to find their own way. This includes career, love, and where they live and work.

Regardless of the differences in these perspectives, however, many families expect their children to follow the family script. Such scripts could include that the past three generations were surgeons or professional athletes, that everyone lived in the Midwest, or that everyone drove a certain type of car. These expectations are explicitly communicated to family members, just like the expectation to become a medical doctor was communicated to Nia.

Nia, however, had a dual perspective. She was Nigerian in her family background and cultural experiences, and American in her place of birth, education, and life experiences. Over the years, she found herself thinking about literature and what makes certain businesses successful. She had friends who were taking classes she thought were interesting, but she didn't believe she could take those courses herself. She didn't think her parents would punish her or do anything negative to her, but she was afraid she would disappoint them and fail the family.

It's natural to feel loyal to those who've cared for us and loved us throughout our entire life. We usually want to follow their lead or desires. In general, love includes giving to the extent that it might feel like a sacrifice to meet the needs of those we care about. This gesture of love, sacrifice, and giving is an important part of connection that unites us as family and helps us thrive together.

At the same time, we have to monitor ourselves to make sure we don't go beyond an appropriate level of sacrifice to a level that abandons our own thoughts, values, and needs. Finding this balance can be tricky, which is why we often need help in the process.

Nia came to me for help because she was trying to find this balance. She knew how important it was to help other family members and how her own mother had sacrificed her dreams of becoming an architect to get a reliable job that would support the family. If Nia chose her own path, would that mean she had done something wrong? How could she tell her parents she didn't want to do what they wanted her to do? How could she "betray" them and go against their wishes? How could she do something different from what was prescribed by the family script?

These were the questions and concerns that swirled around in her mind.

Family Scripts

We all have family scripts that are embedded in us like fingerprints or DNA. They form our values, work ethic, thoughts about education, money, and love, whether we believe in a higher power, and so much more. They shape our world. And just like our fingerprints, each family has a unique script. For example, if the history is that family time is important, the script might say that a good family eats dinner together. Let's look at other family histories and the scripts that might go along with them. You'll find these online at www. IGiveMyselfPermission.com/downloads.

History: *Addiction*

Script: *Our family can hold our liquor. Everyone in our family drinks.*

History: *Being fit*

Script: *Our family exercises regularly and eats healthy food.*

History: *Illness*

Script: *Our family dies early. Everyone has some disease.*

History: *Divorce*

Script: *We are not good at relationships. No need to get married, because it will end in a divorce or breakup.*

History: *Education*

Script: *We are lifelong learners. College (and maybe more) is a must for our family.*

History: *Being there for each other*

Script: *We look out for each other. We sacrifice for our family.*

History: *Building*

Script: *We use our hands and skills to make and fix things. We are DIY people.*

History: *Being in the military or police*

Script: *We serve our country. We sacrifice for the community.*

Family scripts are complicated. On the one hand, they can help connect family members and sometimes even give the family an identity, such as a "giving family," a "family that serves our country," or a "family that overcomes obstacles." On the other hand, family scripts can have a negative aspect; for example, "Most of my family members got divorced, and the ones who stay married are unhappy." This script can lead us to believe that we can't have a long-lasting relationship. Other scripts about a family's struggles with debt or mismanagement of money can cause us to believe the same will happen to us, or a family's history with wealth and status could make us believe there's pressure to act and be a certain way in the family.

These scripts create narratives about families that shape how we see ourselves and our future. While they can influence our behaviors and the narratives we create about ourselves, they aren't true indicators of what we can accomplish in our lives. In fact, many times, we have to acknowledge that our family script is a limiting and inaccurate representation of how we want to live. We then have to fight against the strong current to create a new script.

If there has been a history of drug addiction in your family, for example, there will be a strong influence for you to use, misuse, or abuse substances or find another form of addiction to cope with life's challenges. It's important to know that while your family maintains that script, you can find ways to live your life without addiction. These could include going to therapy, attending addiction programs, facing your trauma, learning new ways to cope, and actively fighting against the many triggers you will face throughout your life. In doing that, you create a new family script and break the cycle of the old one.

That's what Nia was trying to do. When she started working with me, she could only acknowledge the strong influence of her family script. She felt the pressure to do exactly what her parents asked of her without questioning it. She felt like she would have to freely give up her time, resources, knowledge, information, dreams, and desires to serve the family.

Our work together helped Nia acknowledge that this was a family script that many people in her family felt strongly about. But not everyone in the family accepted it. Some rejected it harshly, but few found a way to create a new script. Over time, she realized that she wanted to choose her own professional path while also finding ways to help the family without sacrificing her own well-being.

Nia went on to do just that by giving herself permission to let go of her family's script. There are times she still feels pulled to support the family in ways that may be harmful to her, but through our check-ins, she reestablishes her center and pushes through the uncomfortable feelings. Then she can communicate honestly with her family.

What family scripts have you felt compelled to follow, even if they have gone against your own dreams and desires? For many of us, these scripts are so ingrained in our life and family culture that they can be difficult to recognize. Some are invisible, and the only way to change them or even acknowledge them is with help from a therapist, coach, or friend. Who might help you see, acknowledge, reflect on, and change your family scripts?

Scripts Outside the Family

The scripts that shape our narratives, behaviors, thoughts, and career paths come not only from our families but also from the outside world. We receive constant messages about what it means to be a man, a woman, someone from our ethnic group, someone who is wealthy or poor or from a certain neighborhood, in certain occupations, or unemployed.

There are scripts for everything, and when we hold multiple roles or identities, those scripts can be layered. A woman who is Indian-Asian and works as a computer analyst, for example, may encounter many societal scripts that shape the narratives she forms about herself.

Yes, these scripts from the outside world can also be connected to stereotypes. What we expect from women or someone from a certain country or with a particular identity can be linked to ethnic stereotypes and gender roles. These stereotypes and roles can limit us and sometimes make us hold back our gifts and talents. That's what happened to me. I was restricted by the stereotypes of being an American-born heterosexual Black man of Caribbean (Jamaican) background.

During one of my graduate school breaks when I was in my early twenties and learning to become a therapist, I went home to see my parents. We lived in a two-family home; my parents lived in the first-floor unit, and my uncle, aunt, and cousins lived in the second-floor unit. One of my cousins, who was nine years younger and like a younger brother to me, came downstairs to welcome me and greeted my father with a kiss on the cheek. I was awestruck by this moment. Before this, I couldn't ever remember seeing my father kiss another man, nor could I remember him kissing me, or vice versa. I thought, *How can my cousin kiss my father, and I can't?* I was filled with scripts and narratives that men don't kiss other men, even on the cheek, and that the men in my family don't kiss each other. It was my internalized homophobic fear from societal scripts, coupled with a family script of how men should act within our family.

After reflecting on what was holding me back, I was determined to give myself permission to let go of those limitations. I wanted to be able to kiss my father and not be limited by scripts, narratives, fears, and stereotypes. It wasn't as easy as flipping a switch, of course. I had to give myself permission to go through the process. It took deliberate, intentional work to acknowledge and then let go of the scripts that kept me from connecting with my father in that way.

The truth is that I was more open to changing this family script after years of education, supervision, coaching, and support from others, where I learned a lot about myself, family dynamics, stereotypes, and the process of change. The trigger that helped me see it in myself was observing my cousin as he kissed my father. What moment will trigger you to see the family or societal scripts that are limiting you?

In my case, the scripts and narratives didn't just disappear because I was ready to give myself permission. I came up with a plan, rehearsed it multiple times, and then finally decided I was ready to kiss my father. It appears to be a very simple act, but at that moment, it was a major event. When the day for me to leave approached, I decided I would kiss my father good-bye. That way, if it didn't happen or if he had a negative reaction, I would be able to leave and take some time to process it all.

Well, after telling myself I could do it and taking some deep breaths, I went to kiss my dad on the cheek and completely missed. I ended up kissing him on his ear, but I did it. Now, I laugh whenever I talk about it. But giving myself permission to do that changed my interactions, affection, and bond with my father for another fifteen years until he passed away.

After the ear kiss, every time I saw or left him, I kissed him. We never spoke about it, but he never stopped me. It unlocked a deeper level of intimacy between us that I carried into other relationships, especially the ones with my own children.

It changed my family script around affection and how men can connect. Now, I'm a father of two children—a girl and a boy. I kiss them both multiple times a day. My son has always experienced his father kissing him, and the new family script is that all family members kiss each other regardless of gender.

Wrapping Up

What family script do you need to give yourself permission to let go of? Your courage in releasing an unhealthy script could lead to the birth of a new healthy one that changes your family for generations to come.

Reflect on the spoken or unspoken rules and expectations from your family that have carried over into your adulthood. You can download these questions at www.IGiveMyselfPermission.com/downloads.

- What are the spoken and unspoken scripts from your culture and community that you carried into adulthood?

- Which family scripts hold you back from what you truly want in your life?

- What do you feel pressured to do that you don't want to do?

- What are you pressuring others to do, like your children or other family members, that they don't want to do?

- What societal scripts have you received from the outside world that have influenced your behavior?

- What can you do when giving yourself permission becomes uncomfortable? Who will support you?

- What family scripts do you want to create for future generations?

Chapter 7

I Give Myself Permission to Face My Trauma and Heal

Your trauma is not your fault, but your healing is your responsibility.

—Unknown

T
he very first time I shared my "I Give Myself Permission" presentation was in October 2021 in Colorado Springs to a group of veterans on a self-care retreat. The session was very powerful. The attendees told many vulnerable stories about their lives, and at some point, they all released the heaviness of their past through tears. The session was supposed to be forty-five minutes, but as people opened up and spoke more freely, the organizer gave me the "keep going" sign. Two hours later, we ended our restorative and transformative time with this amazing group of people.

A woman named Kate was one of the attendees. As I was speaking, I noticed that she left the room and spent some time outside. After the talk, she expressed her appreciation to me and revealed that she had stepped out to take a breather.

Confronting the obstacles that keep us from giving ourselves permission can be overwhelming. On some level, that's why we don't do it. It can feel easier to just not give ourselves the permission we long for. To step beyond those limitations, we have to directly address the narratives that created the limitations in the first place.

When people attend my talk and start to face those narratives, challenging parts of their history come to the surface. This isn't easy work and often requires help, support, accountability, affirmations, faith, and more. That's what happened to Kate. Our two-hour session brought her back to experiences in her life that had been traumatic and had caused her to live with limitations.

Six months later, I was sharing my "I Give Myself Permission" message with a group of leaders, entrepreneurs, CEOs, and executive directors in Phoenix. Kate, who is also a leader, was invited to that meeting. She knew that I would be there.

She was determined to show up, and she was on a mission. During the part where I ask people to tell about the social stressors that impact them most and create limitations in their life, Kate raised her hand. I will never forget what happened after I called on her. "I was in the audience when you shared in Colorado Springs," she said, "and I wanted to share but couldn't. Since then, I kept thinking about why I didn't share and told myself if I had another opportunity, I would. So I came here to express what's been impacting me." With tears streaming down her face, she continued, "When I was younger, I was sexually assaulted, and I'm almost fifty. I can't believe it's impacted me for so long. I never shared that part of my life, but after hearing you before, I knew for me, I had to give myself permission to share, face my trauma, and heal."

Kate's bravery and determination changed the atmosphere in that room. It was about more than just sharing about her sexual assault in the past. It was about her willingness to fight through everything that kept her captive, including her voice, to speak in a safe space and reclaim her power.

Many of us experience trauma, and the road to healing can look different for each person. One thing that's consistent, however, is the importance of giving ourselves permission to reclaim our power from the effects of the trauma and the thing or person who traumatized us. That is what Kate did in Phoenix.

Through reclaiming her power and voice, she modeled it for others and inspired them to give themselves permission to do the same. Healing from trauma is what this chapter is all about.

How are you using your voice? Have you started to give yourself permission to take back your power from your trauma?

Is Trauma What I Went Through?

More people have experienced pain, trauma, and abuse than we realize. The data is overwhelming. In May 2024, the World Health Organization said that over 70 percent of people will experience a traumatic event during their lifetime. In most settings, if you look to your left and your right, two of the three of you will have experienced a trauma of some kind. As a result, most of us are dealing with, trying to recover from, or have healed from some type of trauma.

But what exactly is trauma? The American Psychological Association (n.d.) definition states:

> "Trauma is an emotional response to a terrible event like an accident, crime, natural disaster, physical or emotional abuse, neglect, experiencing or witnessing violence, death of a loved one, war, and more. Immediately after the event, shock and denial are typical. Longer term reactions include unpredictable emotions, flashbacks, strained relationships, and even physical symptoms like headaches or nausea."

Various types of abuse, assault, bullying, injustice, injury, witnessing injury, or threat can all be experienced as trauma. Multiple people can experience the same thing but have varying degrees of trauma. One person could feel like what they went through was a life-altering moment that keeps them stuck in an emotional rut. Someone else who went through the same thing could feel like it was challenging but not particularly traumatic. What you experience and how you label it is what's important, not what others say it is or "should" be.

Sometimes, others will want to downgrade your experience of trauma, saying it was only a small challenge. But giving yourself permission to heal from your trauma starts with being able to say that what you experienced was traumatic, even if others disagree.

Of course, not every challenging moment we have in life is traumatic, but maybe we could better recognize the experiences that are indeed traumatic if we didn't allow other people to convince us otherwise. So, at first, give yourself permission to accept that what you experienced might have been trauma.

Victim Blaming Is Real

Historically, the field of psychology has concluded that someone or something is the reason for our psychological distress, abnormalities, diagnosis, or personality flaws. There's a lot of truth to the notion that the pain we experience has something to do with another person and/or a societal challenge. In addition, however, what we do and say and how we make sense of what happened to us also contributes to our condition.

In the early days of psychology, there was a strong belief that to understand and possibly heal our mental health challenges, we had to revisit our past. (This belief is still reflected in present-day psychoanalytical and object relations theories, for example). Austrian neurologist and founder of psychoanalysis Sigmund Freud (1997) believed that our behaviors were based on thoughts and impulses in our unconscious mind. He believed that many factors contributed to what might be in our unconscious, including repressed sexual desires. If we successfully navigated what he termed the "psychosexual stages of development," we could improve our mental health.

Freud is world renowned for his theories and approach, and his methods have been discussed and debated for close to a century. One of these approaches that has been debated involves his thoughts about trauma, especially as experienced by women. In *Trauma and Recovery*, Dr. Judith Herman (1997) discusses a pivotal moment in Dr. Freud's career that added to our perceptions about women, trauma, and child sexual abuse.

Through his studies, Freud discovered that many of his female patients had experienced sexual abuse in childhood. These same women were also diagnosed with hysteria, which was commonly blamed on their being highly emotional. It was considered a physical illness but was also included in the second edition (1968–1980) of the *Diagnostic and Statistical Manual of Mental Disorders* (DSM-2) for psychology until it was finally removed in 1980. (Yes, it was that recent!)

When Freud recognized this correlation, he hypothesized that hysteria was a trauma response and that there was a high number of women who experienced sexual abuse throughout their lifetime, as well as many who experienced sexual abuse as children. He published his findings in his paper *The Aetiology of Hysteria* (1896) and was one of the first to say what we now believe to be true—that many women and men have experienced trauma and abuse, which has had significant mental health repercussions in their lives.

After Freud went public with his thoughts, he realized that abuse and trauma didn't just impact people in a particular neighborhood or those in a lower economic class. It affected those considered to be in the upper class as well. He knew his findings would hold everyone accountable, including the people he wanted to work with. This was important because his career was building, and he was starting to work with the bourgeoisie, which included business owners and people who were influential and wealthy. Having their support would help his career, while alienating them by calling some of them child sexual abusers could destroy it. In an about-face, he retracted his findings and stated that the abuse and trauma might be more closely related to repressed sexual desires. His overt victim blaming added to the narrative that abuse and trauma were a result of something the person did to themselves (in this case, women) versus something that was done *to* them.

I would love to say that as a society, we have learned from our mistakes and now believe the stories of victims of abuse. Unfortunately, we have only found more and more ways to blame victims rather than listen to them. In my years of practice, I have heard countless clients share that when they told their story, someone didn't believe them and thought they were lying.

It becomes extremely hard to give yourself permission when you are dealing with trauma, feel alone, and worry that others won't believe you. But that doesn't mean you should stop trying. Your experience, trauma, or abuse are real even if others doubt you. Others might blame you or try to insinuate that you did something to make it happen, but that is *not* the case. You didn't do anything to deserve a traumatic and/or abusive experience. No one deserves that. Giving yourself permission to heal from your trauma includes knowing that your experience is reality and that nothing you did means you deserved it, regardless of what anyone else might say. They are simply wrong.

A Pause for Self-Care

Before we continue, let's take a moment to slow down and make sure you take good care of yourself. This chapter can be triggering for those who have experienced trauma.

In order to heal, you must first acknowledge and sometimes relive the trauma. That can be difficult, so many people avoid it at all costs. Unfortunately, trauma can still be intrusive with thoughts, memories, and flashbacks. Often, people drink, use substances, keep themselves busy, meditate, dissociate, pray, overeat, isolate, gamble, and do all sorts of other things to avoid dealing with their trauma. Meditation and praying are, of course, healthy behaviors, but not if we use them to avoid underlying pain.

So, avoidance isn't really avoidance. It only allows the effects of the trauma to become worse. Unfortunately, it's almost impossible to heal from trauma without going through the memories of the experience.

I understand that as you have been reading this chapter, you may very well have begun to have traumatic memories. What are you feeling in your body as you read these pages? Do you feel any changes in your emotions? Do you feel overwhelmed, sad, angry, or helpless?

If so, here are some strategies you can use to help you in your healing journey and as you continue reading:

- Take a few deep breaths. A common practice to help destress after a trauma trigger is box breathing or 4x4 breathing. This includes inhaling for a count of four, holding your breath for a count of four, exhaling for a count of four, and holding your breath again for a count of four. Once you complete a full round, repeat it three more times for a total of four rounds (Cleveland Clinic 2021).

- Take a break from reading, and maybe go for a walk. Then come back to continue reading.

- Take a break, bring this book to your next therapy session, read it with your therapist, and share what comes up for you.

- Combine the process of giving yourself permission to heal from your trauma with working with a therapist who practices EMDR (eye movement desensitization and reprocessing).

From Shame to Healing

Shame is a common feeling after experiencing trauma. Without intervention, shame can try to take over your life, showing up daily to make you feel insecure and devalued. Shame can also try to influence you to dim your light and can increase your sadness and depression.

Shame from trauma makes you wonder if you deserve what happened. It can cause you to replay the incident(s) over and over in your mind or to feel that you are less valuable than others. It can cause you to think that you're the only one to have had this experience and possibly make you feel like you should count yourself out.

When you give yourself permission to heal from your trauma, you recognize that shame wants you to believe a false narrative. Yes, the trauma happened to you, but again, it wasn't your fault. Your voice, ideas, presence, and contribution to the world are needed.

Even with all of her accomplishments, Kate struggled with her value and would shrink in important moments in her life. The first time she heard me share about giving yourself permission, she realized that the shame she felt had constantly attempted to silence her. Internally, she wanted to speak up, but the shame made her think no one would hear her or support her.

When she heard my presentation for the second time, she took the emotional leap and found comfort from those around her. Her experiences were validated instead of questioned. All the years of listening to the shame narrative disappeared the moment she gave herself permission to share her story. This was a significant continuation of Kate's healing journey.

Telling your story, using your voice, and reclaiming your power can happen in multiple ways. Healing could look like allowing yourself to have fun, letting go of hurtful/harmful connections, helping others who have experienced trauma, allowing people to get close to you, allowing yourself to be vulnerable with others, and possibly a combination of these. Healing doesn't mean you never feel pain, sadness, or hurt because of the trauma. But that trauma ceases to take over your day, week, month, or life the way it used to.

The healing process could include some or all of these steps: (1) acknowledging that you've experienced something hurtful, harmful, or traumatic; (2) seeking help, which could include talking to a therapist and consulting a medical doctor if there are physical symptoms; (3) journaling about your healing journey; and (4) sharing your story with others, starting with people you trust and whom you know will support you.

The fourth step was Kate's process. She found new joy in her life and in her connections after giving herself permission to heal.

Wrapping Up

Know that the trauma you experienced should never have happened, and that trauma shouldn't continue to steal aspects of your life. Healing doesn't erase the trauma, but it gives you your life back. Of course, it's a journey, not the flipping of a switch, so start today. Give yourself permission to heal from your trauma. You can download these questions at www.IGiveMyselfPermission.com/downloads.

- Have you ever wanted to share something after being inspired but told yourself no or that no one wanted to hear your story?

- Who do you turn to when something challenging, difficult, or traumatic happens to you?

- Have you ever felt like you missed your moment and hoped you would get another chance? Then when the second chance comes, do you take advantage of it like Kate did?

- What role has trauma played in your life?

- When others discredit your trauma or experience, what do you do?

- Have others blamed you for the challenging and traumatic things that have happened to you?

- What are you ashamed of? What role has shame played in your life?

- Where are you in the healing process? Have you:
    - acknowledged that you have experienced something hurtful, harmful, or traumatic;

- sought help, such as talking to a therapist or consulting a medical doctor if there are physical symptoms;

- journaled about your healing journey;

- shared your story with others, starting with people you trust and whom you know will support you?

• What does giving yourself permission to heal from your trauma look like for you? Think about what you avoid talking about and give yourself permission to feel your feelings of grief, anger, hurt, pain, or whatever comes up for you. Do this in the presence of a therapist if you feel too afraid to do it while alone.

• What would your life look like if you didn't believe the false narratives that shame tries to tell you?

- Start by making a list of the narratives that you think about.

- Decide which ones are false or true.

• Write positive affirming narratives to counter each one that is false; for example, "My trauma happened because I went out and should have stayed home." That's a false narrative. The trauma happened because someone did or said something that was harmful. As a positive affirmation, you can say, "I can go out to be with friends or stay in; it is my choice," or "I am working through my trauma and will continue to gain back my power to do what's best for me."

Chapter 8

I Give Myself Permission to Forgive

*Forgiveness is not an occasional act; it is
a constant attitude.*

—Dr. Martin Luther King Jr.

It may be a cliché that forgiving others is more for us than it is for them, but it's true. When we don't forgive, we spend more mental and emotional energy on the person who wronged us than we do on our own happiness and well-being. Yes, I know forgiving is easier said than done. When we've been wronged, hurt, betrayed, or experienced an injustice, our mind and emotions focus on the other person and what they did to us.

We sometimes think about what we'd like to say or do the next time we see them. Some people even think about revenge. While this is a perfectly normal reaction, it's incredible and inspiring to see someone experience a harsh and tragic event in life because of someone else and still find a way to give themselves permission to forgive. Let's talk about a remarkable act of forgiveness.

Leon Ford, author and activist, joined me on my podcast, LEAPcast, in June 2022, about a year before the release of his book, *An Unspeakable Hope: Brutality, Forgiveness, and Building a Better Future for My Son* (Ford 2023). He shared his journey toward giving himself permission to forgive and be the best version of himself.

One online description for Leon's book says: "In 2012, nineteen-year-old Leon Ford was shot five times by a Pittsburgh police officer during a racially charged traffic stop stemming from a case of mistaken identity. When he woke up in the hospital, he was faced with two life-changing realities: he was a new father, and he was paralyzed from the waist down. Leon found the only way to move forward was to let go of his bitterness and learn to practice forgiveness."

When the police pulled Leon over, they automatically assumed he was a suspect because of his race, and they thought he had a weapon. But he wasn't armed, and he hadn't committed a crime. When he woke up after having been shot multiple times, he was handcuffed to a hospital bed.

To say the least, this was a traumatic experience that involved racial injustice, gun violence, and paralysis. While Leon was in the hospital, his girlfriend at the time was simultaneously giving birth to their son. He was unable to be there for that birth because he was still viewed as a suspect. Then he learned that he would never walk again.

So many things happened at the same time, from being mistreated because he's a Black man to being shot to missing the birth of his son to becoming paralyzed. The compound impact of everything pushed Leon into an emotional tailspin that included sadness, depression, anger, rage, isolation, and suicidal thoughts. Family and friends tried to support him, but pain and hate consumed him until, one day, he decided he couldn't continue like that. He started therapy and began letting others care for him. Over time, he regained his confidence with a renewed sense of purpose.

Leon knew he could make a difference with his words, platform, and actions. He openly talked about his journey and the healing process. Then he did something that shocked everyone. He knew he wouldn't be able to live the life he desired, be the father he wanted to be, or truly make an impact if he didn't forgive the police officers who shot him.

He wanted his son to have a better life than he did, but to make that possible, Leon knew he had to change. He increased his practice of mindfulness and gratitude, and he examined all parts of his life, not just the gun violence he had experienced. He gave himself permission to forgive the officers internally and publicly. Then he decided to meet with them in person. The meeting was canceled and rescheduled multiple times by the officers until it finally happened. This face-to-face meeting led to the development of a genuine connection and, eventually, a collaboration.

Together, Leon and the man who had been police chief at the time of the shooting formed a nonprofit organization called the Hear Foundation (www.hearfoundation.com). Its mission is to convene, fund, and implement initiatives that build police and resident relationships, strengthening Pittsburgh's neighborhoods. The goal of this collaboration is to help heal the community by bringing together leaders, Pittsburgh police, and residents to create a safe and thriving place for everyone.

Leon knew that his act of forgiveness was necessary for him to move forward in his life, but establishing the foundation would also help the community forgive. Many people in his city and across the country were still angry and scared, and didn't want more racially charged incidents to happen in their city or the country. The foundation would allow his personal journey of forgiveness to become a bridge to community forgiveness and healing.

Forgiveness Is a Process

Forgiveness is the act of releasing our emotional, physical, financial, and/or spiritual pain. It's the process of getting to the place where we can say we don't hate the person who wronged us and that we aren't angry with them anymore.

For some people, forgiveness is a reconciliation process that reconnects friends, family members, business partners, and romantic partners. For others, it releases the offending person, but the result doesn't have to be friendship or even any kind of connection at all. We can forgive and go our separate ways.

It's important to realize that giving yourself permission isn't like flipping a switch. It's a process. There's a back-and-forth we go through in our mind and emotions. We may wonder if we're doing the right thing, if we're being weak, if it will matter, or even how long it will take.

But giving yourself permission to forgive doesn't mean you forget that something negative happened. Leon will never forget being shot or that it resulted in his paralysis. He will always remember what happened to him and how it happened. But he made a conscious choice to forgive the people responsible for his pain.

The goal isn't to forget. Remembering what happened can sometimes provide motivation in other areas of life. For Leon, remembering what happened fueled his ability to be an advocate for others and become an activist against injustice.

Don't Let Resentment Steal Your Future

When someone does something to hurt, harm, or offend us, the pain we feel as a result usually turns into resentment, which becomes our weapon to try to protect ourselves from further pain. But it doesn't work the way we think it will. In fact, our resentment can be so intense that everyone feels it, including the people who love us and who want to be there for us. It can end up pushing people away, even when they're trying to offer support.

The goal is to not let resentment steal our future. We have to give ourselves permission to follow the path of forgiveness instead.

Now let's look at a second remarkable act of forgiveness. In January 2023, Damion Cooper, CEO of Project Pneuma (www.projectpneuma.org), joined me on my podcast and shared his powerful story of giving himself permission to forgive and be his authentic self.

That's what Damion chose to do, but it wasn't easy. At twenty years old, he was in college on an athletic wrestling scholarship. He had just finished wrestling practice and decided to go home and visit his family for a home-cooked meal. He didn't have a car at the time, so he took two buses to get close to his house. After getting off the last bus, he walked through a high-crime neighborhood and was almost home when he turned around to see two guys standing behind him. One of them pulled out a gun and shot Damion one inch above the heart. After ricocheting multiple times, cracking his sternum, breaking three ribs, and puncturing his lung, the bullet finally lodged in the nerves under his right arm.

Somehow, he was able to get to the door of his house, and his stepdad brought him inside. After the shock wore off, Damion started to feel the pain. As he was bleeding profusely, his mom rocked him back and forth, his sister screamed, and his stepdad held him.

When two police officers arrived, one of them accused Damion of being involved in a crime and asked if the shooting was an act of retaliation. Eventually, they started to help him until the paramedics arrived. With the assistance of neighborhood firefighters, they were able to get him out of the house. He felt the tug of his eyes closing, and one of the paramedics said, "Baby, if you close your eyes, you won't be able to open them back up. Focus on the streetlights and count them."

Damion had surgery and endured a lengthy recovery, during which he became depressed. The doctors informed him that he wouldn't be able to wrestle again, which meant he would lose his scholarship. He lost a lot of weight, and he couldn't shower or go to the bathroom on his own. He felt emasculated, stopped believing in God, and stopped talking to people. He was full of resentment and constantly wondered, *Why me? What did I do to deserve this?* He was afraid to go out of the house because he didn't know who had shot him and if they were going to come back. He struggled with depression, sadness, despair, and anxiety for years.

About four years later, Damion was at his lowest and contemplated taking his life on a particular New Year's Eve. Before he could do anything, two friends came over and invited him to church. On the way, they drove by the same neighborhood where he had been shot. He immediately relived the trauma.

During the church service, the minister spoke directly to Damion. He recalls: "That night was December 31, 1996. That came out to be four years, two months, and eighteen days since I was shot, and it felt like it was the first time that someone heard me." This experience of feeling heard and seen empowered Damion to give himself permission to release the pain, depression, hurt, loss, and resentment. He even released a loud cry.

That moment changed his future. During that church service, with tears and mucus coming down his face, he decided to forgive the person who shot him. Without knowing who the person was, he knew he had to release everything, including resentment and forgiveness.

Damion later went on to finish college, then went to seminary and started volunteering in a prison ministry. During his time there, he mentored young men, helping them develop life skills and find resources to transition from being incarcerated to being released.

Without knowing it, he started to mentor the young man who shot him. After a sit-down conversation in the prison with a correctional officer and chaplain watching, the young man shared that he had shot someone on their way home. Damion realized in that moment who the young man was and said, "You shot me." He walked over to the young man and showed his wound. Then he said, "I forgive you." They both proceeded to cry.

The Power of Forgiveness

The young man was later released from prison, got involved in the church, got married, and had two daughters. He has said that receiving mentorship and forgiveness from Damion helped change his life. These two men have also stayed connected with each other.

Because Damion gave himself permission to forgive and let go of the resentment, he not only was able to heal from the trauma he endured, but his forgiveness also helped the young man who shot him, as well as others around both of them.

It may take some time, but if we never work toward forgiveness, we're likely to hold on to our grudges forever. It's a complex process that almost always requires intentionality. It starts with a thought, when we tell ourselves that we will forgive the other person. We have to mentally go there first. Then we must say it aloud. When we do that, it becomes more real.

Lastly, we must live it as best we can, which means actively reminding ourselves that we forgave the other person. It also helps to remind ourselves that forgiveness means giving ourselves permission to focus on our future rather than our past.

In the beginning, we might have to remind ourselves multiple times a day, but eventually, it will become a part of our life. This is what Damion did and what you can do, too, when you give yourself permission to forgive.

Self-Forgiveness

The most difficult kind of forgiveness for most people is self-forgiveness. We may blame ourselves for mistakes we've made or for not being perfect. Perhaps we flunked a class, trusted the wrong person, or did something that hurt someone we love. Sometimes we may go through a rough patch (we could be depressed, feeling overwhelmed, or anxious, or just not in the best place) in which we make a series of mistakes or bad choices.

Some of those mistakes might be serious ones that could result in losing your job, the end of a relationship or friendship, a car accident, being incarcerated, disconnecting from a family member, and countless other situations. Other people might never actually see the severity of the internal pain you feel as a result of what you did. I have worked with clients who betrayed the trust of their partner, a family member, teammates, or colleagues, and rebuilding the trust is a very long and challenging process. This all leads to feeling that you cannot give yourself permission to forgive yourself.

When we hurt people we care about, do something that's not consistent with our values, or have multiple situations where we feel like we failed, our inner thoughts can make us believe that we *are* our mistakes instead of someone who had a moment (or moments) when they made a decision that wasn't the best. Unfortunately, we repeat the incident or situation in our heads over and over. We rehearse the parts we feel bad about and then the negative self-talk adds to the shame and guilt. We say hurtful and harmful things to ourselves, which strengthens the dichotomous narrative that we are bad while others are good. The narrative that you are "less than" or "not good enough" may replay over and over, digging you deeper into self-blame. You might feel that you don't deserve to be happy, or you may not trust yourself to make good decisions.

The truth is that the harsh and negative narratives you are telling yourself are false. Your mistakes and bad choices are not the full sum of who you are. They don't define you. Yes, there could be a pattern that you have to identify, and maybe some support could help you stop that pattern. But the pattern doesn't mean you are less than, damaged, discarded, and not worthy of being forgiven by someone else or by yourself.

Self-forgiveness is a beautiful and necessary act of kindness and love that you can give yourself. Shame, rehearing negative self-talk, and punishing yourself usually result in continuing negative patterns while decreasing the amount of self-love you give to yourself. Your family, partner, friends, and colleagues want you to love yourself and value the version of yourself that doesn't hold on to so much shame. Giving yourself permission to forgive yourself is necessary in order to move forward in your life.

Here are some ways you can start the process of self-forgiveness:

- Be honest with yourself about what you did or said.

- Reflect on what influenced you to do it.

- Ask for forgiveness from the person you hurt. (If they forgive you, great. Now you can do the same. If they don't forgive you, that doesn't mean you can't forgive yourself.)

- Remind yourself that in spite of what happened, it's okay to practice self-compassion.

- Get help from a therapist, coach, or trusted friend.

- Read books and listen to podcasts about ways to quiet the negative self-talk while increasing your self-love.

- Give yourself permission to forgive yourself.

Repeat as many of the steps above until you start to live a life of self-forgiveness.

Promoting Forgiveness

This section provides a variety of ways to promote forgiveness.

Write a forgiveness letter. It could be to someone you would like to ask forgiveness from, or it could be to yourself to practice self-forgiveness. The act of writing a letter or journaling your letter could be therapeutic because it allows you to express your emotions and release resentment. Share the letter with your therapist and/or a trusted person in your life. At this point, you don't have to send it to the person you are seeking forgiveness from.

Develop a list of forgiveness-related affirmations. For example, (1) *I am more than the mistake(s) I made. It's okay for me to accept forgiveness.* (2) *The pain I feel is real, but not forgiving will keep the pain inside.*

Write a list of the thoughts that keep you from forgiving yourself or someone else.

Reflect on how it felt when someone forgave you or on the last time you witnessed forgiveness.

Role-play. If you plan to forgive someone or ask for forgiveness, role-play it with your therapist or a trusted person. Practice what you will say multiple times until you feel more comfortable.

Practice mindfulness. Pay attention to your breath, your body, and your emotions when you think about forgiveness, when you ask for forgiveness, and when you offer forgiveness.

Wrapping Up

Take some time to reflect on the following questions. Then take out your journal and write down your thoughts. At www. IGiveMyselfPermission.com/downloads, you can download these questions; you'll also find a list of tools for self-forgiveness and ways to promote forgiveness.

- What makes forgiveness difficult for you?

- What would you do if you faced the person who hurt you?

- Would you be able to give yourself permission to forgive after the unspeakable happens to you or to someone you care about?

- Do you think forgiving someone is a sign of weakness?

- Are you holding resentment or unforgiveness toward anyone?

- Could your act of forgiveness create a ripple effect in the lives of people around you?

- What did you learn about forgiveness from the stories about Leon and Damion?

- Is there anyone you need to ask to forgive you?

- Are you struggling to forgive yourself for something you did?

- What negative narratives are keeping you from forgiving yourself?

Chapter 9

I Give Myself Permission to Play and Rest

We don't stop playing because we grow old; we grow old because we stop playing.

—George Bernard Shaw

When we're younger, going fast, jumping high, and running into things all seem like fun. But as we get older, we see this as reckless and we begin calculating possible risks. Our minds are filled with fear and anxiety about what could go wrong, or we worry that others will judge us. Before we know it, fun, play, and excitement are limited experiences that we might explore only once a year on a vacation.

I hear stories like these all the time from CEOs and executives, stay-at-home parents, and people with multiple jobs. Those of us who want the best for the people we care about often face this challenge. We work hard to meet the needs of those we love while simultaneously doing less for ourselves, including having fun, making time to rest, and generally enjoying life.

One of my executive coaching clients, Leo, is a perfect example of doing so much for others that he has little time left for rest or play. He's a US Marine Corps veteran, community leader, business consultant, father, husband, son, brother, and friend. Everyone looks up to him, and he's the person they seek when they need something. When his phone rings, it's usually someone asking for a favor. It could be help because of a death in the community, a family member in the hospital, a need for money, or a business struggling to meet its financial goals. He also receives everyday requests from his children, parents, and wife.

Leo faithfully served his country, and it's true that service is embedded in his DNA. He often thinks about others and volunteers to help even when people don't ask.

But his unwavering service comes at a cost. Because of this level of responsibility, Leo has a tremendous amount of chronic stress. He rarely gets enough rest, and he often struggles with sleep. He gets up early in the morning to make sure he meets the needs and demands of everyone else, but he has little time for himself. When he attended a leadership program where I shared my "I Give Myself Permission" talk, Leo realized he wasn't giving himself permission to play, rest, or enjoy life.

Since then, it has been life-changing for him to give himself permission to breathe, rest, say no, put himself first, take breaks, and even go on vacation. Leo now goes horseback riding at least four or five times a year. He has also worked on his sleep hygiene (limiting tech and screens before bed, winding down, and practicing mindfulness). He has also given himself permission to travel more. He took an anniversary trip with his wife to Paris, and they also visited Dubai, among other places. He's determined to see the world and have fun wherever he goes.

Leo even likes bringing the "I Give Myself Permission" pillow I gave him on his various trips and taking pictures with it. The pillow has seen the Eiffel Tower and many other iconic places around the world. It's his fun way of reminding himself that he's giving himself permission to put himself first even when multiple people still need something from him.

Leo found a way to give himself permission to both rest and play, while simultaneously learning that his community wouldn't fall apart without him. What about you? Do you give yourself permission to rest and play?

Why Rest and Play Are Important

Are you always in "go" mode? In our society, we can feel pressure to make more money, keep up with others, and work nonstop just to barely stay afloat. The demands to keep going can come from internal or external pressures—from feeling we need to have the latest outfit, car, or gadget, to paying for our children's activities, to paying off debt, to working overtime to pay our rent that's already overdue. The pressure is everywhere. As a result, rest and play often get pushed to the back burner.

Of course, it's easy to believe that rest and play aren't productive. You might have heard that if you want to be taken seriously, you need to spend more time working, doing, and staying busy. Some of you have heard that you need to be *twice* as good or work harder than everyone else if you want to get somewhere. The subtext to these messages is that resting and playing are lazy.

Throughout this book, I have encouraged you to give yourself permission to do many things, such as take risks, be imperfect, live boldly, dream big, heal, forgive, and love, among others. But even with these, if you aren't careful, it can feel like you have to work harder and relinquish time for rest and play.

My belief is that the more we make time to play and rest, the more we're equipped to give ourselves permission in other areas. Play, fun, creativity, music, and theater can release stress and assist the healing process. Play and rest can help us regulate our emotions, communicate our thoughts and feelings, solve problems, come up with new innovations, and become more self-aware.

When we work, add to our to-do lists, volunteer, parent, and love without breaks, we're almost sure to experience burnout, get into arguments, feel less creative/innovative, and give ourselves less permission in the areas we need most. We stay out of balance when we do everything but play and rest.

Play Like a Kid

Kids have a great ability to integrate play into whatever they do. I was recently at an event where there were several children who didn't know each other. Yet within minutes they were running around, playing and chasing each other. Instead of doing nothing, they made new friends and came up with a game.

At an outing in my family, the three children present started playing Duck, Duck, Goose. Usually, this game has a minimum of four players to give them a chance to be surprised and to rest between rounds. But that didn't matter to these three youngsters. They played the game as if nothing were different. As the adult watching, I was amused, but also impressed. They didn't care what others would do, and they didn't care if they had enough people. It was so easy for them to give themselves permission to have fun without following the rules.

Unfortunately, as we get older, we get lost in the details that don't really matter, and we forget how to play. Everything gets in the way, from our schedule to our fears about who's watching. When was the last time you played your favorite card game, ran a race to see who's faster (please stretch first!), told a funny story, played a video game or board game, or just simply played?

It's time we grown-ups gave ourselves permission to play like kids! If the only way you'll do it is to schedule time to play, then schedule it. Do whatever you need to make time for fun. You won't regret it, as it will help you release the stress you've been holding on to. Playing like a kid will bring you joy, allow you to laugh, and inspire creativity and innovation.

Get Your Rest

Sleep is also very important to our well-being. Along with physical activity and healthy eating, sleep is one of the three key ingredients for a healthy life. At the same time, many people struggle in one or all of these areas.

More people than we realize find it difficult to go to sleep or stay asleep. Many people who do get to sleep find that they're restless during the night, tossing and turning. This leaves them still tired in the morning.

In the busyness of life, including the demands at work, home, sport, and community, we push ourselves to extreme limits, often sacrificing sleep and rest. You may get up early to exercise, read, and help the kids so that you can get to work on time. You may stay up late at night to organize the house, check emails, read the book you've been trying to finish, help the kids with homework, finish a work project, scroll through social media, or spend time with your partner—all while pushing your bedtime later and later. Between getting up early and going to bed late, you probably aren't getting enough sleep.

Most of us fail to practice good sleep hygiene. Incorporating these habits into your routine can help you have higher-quality sleep:

- A regular bedtime

- Avoiding screens about thirty minutes before bed

- Avoiding long naps, especially in the evening

- Creating a wind-down routine

- Avoiding late-night snacking

- Limiting caffeine in the afternoon and evening

- Avoiding alcohol before bedtime

What if you gave yourself permission to get more sleep and quality rest? How would that impact your mood, health, and state of mind?

According to the American Psychological Association (2013), there is a relationship between more stress and less sleep. We need quality sleep for our body to reset and for our organs to heal and release toxins. Sleep also decreases anxiety, lowers the stress hormone cortisol, improves our immune system, increases our cognitive skills, and reduces irritability. It recharges our body, mind, and spirit. Without it, we're unable to function optimally.

Saying Yes to Rest and Play May Mean Saying No to Other Things

Giving ourselves permission to rest and play may mean saying no to something else. If we're accustomed to being productive every waking moment, we're saying yes to that while saying no to rest and play. We might even be saying no to activities that have significant meaning for us, such as playing with our kids or spending quality time with our partner.

When we say no to people we care about, we often say yes to work, chores, and responsibilities. Giving ourselves permission to play and rest allows us to introduce more balance into our lives. It's important to learn to say no in order to learn to say yes to what we truly value, cherish, and need for our emotional, physical, financial, and mental well-being.

This applies to all of us, including me. I have been fortunate to give myself permission in many areas of my life, but throughout the course of writing this book, I have recognized areas where I don't give myself permission. One of those was learning to ski. Because of my busy schedule and my fears of getting injured, I have said no to previous opportunities to take skiing lessons. But while writing this book, I was determined not to let my fears and schedule stop me from taking these lessons. My wife also wanted to take skiing lessons, so we signed up for a package together. About six months before we were to start, my schedule started to pick up with speaking engagements. I felt stuck.

I value the opportunity to speak and provide a service, but this was an opportunity for me to give myself permission to have some fun learning to ski. I ended up compromising by splitting the package. I was able to protect my schedule and say no to other opportunities so that I could say yes to the skiing lessons. I attended the first four hours of instruction, but not the last four. Still, I learned enough to make me want to do it again.

Sometimes, in giving yourself permission, you have to start where you can. It isn't an all-or-nothing process. It's almost always a balancing act. I wanted to have fun, learn how to ski, and experience the beautiful outdoors while spending time with my wife. But I couldn't do it fully because I also wanted to say yes to most of my speaking opportunities. So I said no to my schedule to the extent that I could, and yes to fun to the degree that I could. I had a new experience and started to learn a new skill.

The lesson here is to avoid putting so much pressure on yourself to rest and play that you add to your stress level, which would defeat the purpose. Instead, give yourself permission to have fun, play, rest, and sleep, while balancing your responsibilities as best you can. It will never be perfect, which is fine. We have been talking about being imperfect throughout this book. Just remember that the memorable experiences you create with fun and play and the relaxed state of mind you achieve with sleep and rest will help you be at your best for everyone else in your life, as well as working toward your professional goals.

Wrapping Up

Take some time to reflect on the questions below. Then take out your journal, or download the questions at www.IGiveMyself Permission.com/downloads, and write down the thoughts that come from your reflections.

- What challenges do you have with giving yourself permission to rest and sleep?

- What challenges do you have with giving yourself permission to play and have fun?

- What "ball(s)" do you fear you'll drop if you make more time to play and rest?

- What do you need to say no to in order to say yes to play and rest?

- What do you enjoy doing that's playful and fun?

- What provides rest and calm for you?

- When is the next time you can play? Schedule a date this month, ideally this week.

- When is the next time you can rest? Schedule a date this week, ideally for at least a short time each day.

- Create a list of various things you enjoy that are restful and fun for you. This is your rest-and-play toolkit. Scatter these throughout your calendar as appointments with yourself—and keep those appointments!

Chapter 10

I Give Myself Permission to Take Care of Myself

Caring for myself is not self-indulgence,
it is self-preservation, and it is an act of
political warfare.

—Audre Lorde

The pressure to make more money, take care of loved ones, perform religious or civic duties, and work (sometimes even multiple jobs or shifts) can keep us so busy that we run out of time for ourselves. But what does it mean to actually practice self-care? We've already talked about play and rest; now let's go deeper into what self-care truly means.

Many of us think we understand self-care, but we still don't practice it. Even when we know the benefits from past experience, it's still hard to prioritize ourselves. Yet, without self-care, we can handle only so much stress, negativity, anxiety, depression, complaining, and challenge before we're depleted. Without it, we self-destruct, repeat negative and unhealthy patterns, develop illnesses, and sometimes show the worst parts of ourselves to those we love.

It should be easy to make time for self-care, but it isn't, is it? We don't make time for it, and we don't give ourselves permission to make the changes we need to integrate it into our lives.

In an earlier chapter, I introduced you to my mother and shared how hard she worked, sometimes doing double shifts at the hospital to support our family. She was so busy taking care of everyone else that taking care of herself was an afterthought.

Of course, she had no one modeling self-care for her. She was taught that she had to work even on her days off, cleaning, cooking, and organizing at home. If she wasn't doing household chores, she used her day off to pick up an extra shift or engage with her religious community. She didn't spend her time planning self-care retreats, journaling, or going to a spa. It was even hard for her to take time to sleep or sit down and enjoy the environment around her.

We have a narrative in our society that self-care is only for others, wealthy people, those who have nothing better to do, or people who are self-indulgent or have lots of free time. This is simply false.

We're made to believe it's our duty to give to others as much as possible, as if it's the only way we can deserve our existence. While it's wonderful to help others, it's impossible to give from an empty pitcher, so we have to learn to fill up our own pitcher first.

So how do we give ourselves permission to prioritize ourselves when everyone around us says we should put everybody and everything else first?

The Privilege of Self-Care

It's important to acknowledge that the goal is for everyone to actively care for themselves and use effective self-care strategies. At the same time, I acknowledge that self-care can be considered an act of privilege. It's a privilege to have the time, money, and freedom for it. Right now, there's someone who's leaving their first job on their way to their second job. There's someone who wants, maybe even needs, a day off or a mental health day but has to wait for their boss to say yes to it. And their boss keeps saying no. There's someone worrying about having enough money to pay for food for their family.

I know there are numerous barriers that can keep us from taking or making the time to care for ourselves. But you, too, can practice self-care. It starts with telling yourself: *Despite my situation, I give myself permission to care for myself.* Then you'll find ways, no matter how small, to do it. But you'll never do it if you don't start with permission.

Self-Care Is *Our* Care

Most of us don't realize that when we run ourselves into the ground, it has a negative impact on our loved ones, too. Not only does our example teach our children that, when they grow up, they must give and give to the point of exhaustion, but we also run out of juice for our job, friends, and family. We can't give our best when we're spent.

So self-care is more than caring for yourself; it's caring for every-one around you. Each of us is an integral part of our community. Therefore, self-care can be a form of "our-care," as defined by Dr. Shawn Ginwright in *The Four Pivots* (2022). He says that when one of us is sick, it impacts everyone around us. Even if we aren't conta-gious, others may have to take care of us or do the things we usually do and now can't. For that reason alone, it's in our best interest to stay healthy. When *you* are sick, *we* are sick.

The same mindset applies to self-care. If we don't practice it reg-ularly, we contribute to unhealthy norms. We become complicit in systems meant to keep us moving, distracted, and always chasing the next thing. We forfeit the peace, renewal, and mental and physical strength that come from being well cared for.

When we don't practice self-care, we actually have less to give to others. We may lose our temper more easily, fail to spend quality time with the people we love, or just become downright poor company. In short, we can end up sacrificing what we value most.

So it's vital to give ourselves permission to take care of ourselves as much as we do anyone else. Without self-care, we risk losing our ability to fully enjoy the life we've been given.

Self-Care Is More Than Going to the Spa

Many people think of self-care as taking a bath, having a spa day, or going to the nail salon. While these are great things to do, I consider them to be level one self-care practices; they're just scratching the surface. If all we do is focus on a day of pampering here and there, we miss opportunities to truly care for ourselves.

Sometimes, by the time we get to the spa or nail salon, we're so overwhelmed that it's hard to enjoy the experience, and our high stress levels immediately return. We want to get to a place where we have a self-care routine that can provide regular stress reduction while increasing our joy.

At home, I have a feelings wheel in the form of a pillow that I often bring out with my children, asking them to identify what they're feeling. This wheel is a circular chart with emotions in various categories. You can download it at my website: www.IGiveMyself Permission/downloads. When I ask my children to identify their feelings, they often run away, saying, "Oh no! Not the feelings wheel!" When I'm in a silly mood, I chase them around the house with the pillow, saying, "Tell me what you feel!"

All jokes aside, identifying your feelings is a great way to determine the type of self-care you really need.

When I ask my children how they feel, I'm trying to help them know how they can take care of themselves, and I want to know how I can assist them in caring for themselves. What's interesting about the feelings-wheel pillow is that when adults come over, they often look at it and also try to identify their feelings. Sometimes we forget that we have feelings until we have a chart in front of us showing us the many possibilities.

When we don't notice our emotions, we also don't notice we need self-care. So, giving yourself permission to take care of yourself involves diving deeper into your feelings.

For those of you who prefer apps to a chart, you can use the How We Feel app (www.howwefeel.org), which works in a similar way. This app will ask you if you experienced high positive feelings, low positive feelings, high negative feelings, or low negative feelings during the day. After you make your selection, it will bring you a list of feelings similar to what's on my wheel.

I highly recommend trying it out so that you can make the connection between your feelings and how you practice self-care. Perhaps you need to sleep, laugh, journal, cry, or connect with others. Self-care is about taking the time to feel and discover what you need in order to reduce stress and heal.

Self-Care Routines

Near the end of my "I Give Myself Permission" talk, I share my top five self-care practices and encourage the audience to be intentional about creating their own top five. Mine include:

Traveling and looking at pictures from previous trips. I love to travel. Being away is relaxing and fun, and allows for quality time with loved ones. Even when I can't travel, however, looking at pictures from previous trips takes me back to those moments and helps me feel good. It also makes me grateful for those experiences. Connecting with gratitude is a great way to shift emotions from negative to positive.

Deep breaths (refer to chapter 7 for instructions) and time for reflection and prayer. All of these center me, releasing tension and stress. They are meaningful practices that promote calm, slow our heart rate, and help us feel hopeful.

Long walks, hikes, and car rides with my wife while we talk. My friendship with my wife is an important part of our relationship. When we go on long walks, hikes, or car rides, we have fascinating conversations. Plus, doing some kind of physical activity adds to the release of stress and reduction of stress hormones. So exercise and connecting with others are both excellent self-care strategies.

Laughing, sharing stories, and having vulnerable conversations with close friends. Besides connecting with my wife, I love laughing, being silly, and sharing openly with friends. It refuels and energizes me. According to the American Psychological Association (2019), social support is an important way we cope with stressors and challenges.

Evidence is also growing that laughter reduces stress and increases relaxation, both emotionally and physically (Akimbekov and Razzaque 2021).

Massages, pedicures, golf, and "fake" tennis. I call it fake tennis because if you saw me play, you would say, "That's not tennis." But I still enjoy it, as well as golf, massages, and pedicures. They all help me feel better as I care for my body. In terms of golf and tennis, spending time outdoors positively influences my mood and reduces stress.

What's on your list? If you're unsure, you can choose to try some of the suggestions that follow. There are six categories, including personal, physical, professional, spiritual, psychological, and emotional (Phoenix 2013).

Self-Care: Personal

Self-care starts with you. You've likely heard countless times that you should put on your own oxygen mask before you try to help others. You can't help anyone else if you're compromised, ill, or unable to function.

What can you do for you? What are your personal goals? When's the last time you really danced? Is there a friend you miss hanging out with? Do you enjoy sudoku, puzzles, or video games? Do you like taking bubble baths or watching movies by yourself? Whatever it is, put "me time" on your calendar. If any of these activities are challenging for you, start smaller and work your way up. For example, start with an hour or two if you can't take a day, a fifteen-minute walk instead of an hour, one or two hands of a card game if you don't have time for the full game. You can also get support to help you, but make sure you share what would be helpful to you.

Self-Care: Physical

Have you been having back pains or muscle soreness? Do you have a nutrition plan that fits your lifestyle? Physical self-care means taking care of your body's health.

Even if you've neglected your fitness and flexibility for a long time, don't let that stop you from starting, trying, or adding something else to your routine. You could start with walking, or add running or a nightly stretch. Do you have a workout buddy or accountability partner? They can help you stick with it. Do you enjoy running, yoga, Pilates, or dancing?

Changing what you eat or working with a nutritionist to help you design a food plan for yourself can also make a significant difference in how you feel in all aspects of your life.

Physical self-care can also include touch, cuddling, intimacy, and sex. Try that new outfit or new cologne. Flirt with your partner or the person you've been talking to on an app. It might be time to get in the mood, play your favorite playlist, and take Marvin Gaye's advice: let's get it on.

Self-Care: Professional

Have you updated your resume recently or reminded yourself that you're good at what you do? Professional self-care focuses on you, your career, and your work-life balance. Are you working so hard that you don't have time for yourself, your relationship, or your family? Did you go on a vacation in the past year, or do you know when your next vacation will be? When's the last time you had dinner with your family, went on a date, or hung out with friends?

This is a good time to evaluate your time and commitment to work. Of course, there's nothing wrong with working hard, but does your hard work come at the expense of something else? Would you benefit from a mental health day?

I suggest making a list of the people and activities that are important to you and being intentional about including them on your schedule. Maybe it's someone who's been trying to connect with you. Find the time to fit them into your schedule. You could also join a group or attend a conference to connect with colleagues and like-minded people in your industry.

Self-Care: Spiritual

Some people acknowledge a higher power, and others don't believe at all. For those who have some connection to a spiritual practice or belief, it can be an important aspect of self-care.

This could involve praying, meditating, doing a devotional, sharing beliefs with others, or going to a mosque, synagogue, or church. Taking care of your spiritual side can bring peace and calm into your life and perhaps even help you feel safer and more supported. For some people, their spiritual practice guides how they show up in challenging and stressful times. It could be reading a religious text, listening to inspiring music, or being in nature. Embrace that part of you as it could provide the missing part of your self-care routine.

Self-Care: Psychological

Taking care of your mind is as important as taking care of your body. Reading a book, talking openly with a friend, being vulnerable with your partner, and going to therapy are all ways you can practice psychological self-care. If you haven't started, now is a good time.

Anything meditative can be helpful to the psychological part of you. This can include formal meditation, writing in a journal, or working in your garden. Don't minimize the importance of self-care for your mind. There are apps such as Calm, Headspace, and others that help facilitate a mindfulness practice. Maybe it's time to go back to therapy for yourself, your relationship, or your family. Integrating these practices into your work life could reduce your stress at work and help you be more present at home. Self-care doesn't have to be siloed; you can give yourself permission to integrate self-care into every part of your life.

Self-Care: Emotional

Sometimes, when we think of self-care, we think about the physical and personal aspects, such as exercising or going to a spa, while leaving out emotional self-care.

Here's an idea: Has anyone ever asked you to share five things you like about yourself? If so, did you struggle to answer the question, or could you come up with only three? This is one of the reasons why we work on the emotional side of self-care.

If you can't think of five things, you could ask a close friend or family member to tell you what they like about you. Once you have your top five list, write it down on paper or on your phone so that you can refer to it often as a form of self-care. It will be emotionally uplifting whenever you see it. Perhaps make it a routine to review it at the beginning of each week or each day.

You could also start a gratitude practice in the morning or evening to remind you of what you appreciate in your life, including yourself.

When's the last time you wore an outfit and thought, *I look good*, instead of shaming yourself? Pay attention to your self-talk. Do you beat yourself up or chastise yourself a lot? If so, part of self-care is noticing when you do that so you can stop. Make a better choice and begin to speak as kindly to yourself as you do to others.

These are all aspects of emotional self-care that can become a part of your routine without taking a lot of time. Don't underestimate their impact! They can work wonders to help you feel better in general.

Wrapping Up

When we face challenges and adversity in life, it's especially important to practice self-care. And if we already have our favorite self-care techniques in motion, we'll be prepared for the challenging times. Take the time to establish a self-care routine, incorporating your rest and play toolkit from the last chapter.

Giving yourself permission to practice self-care routinely in multiple areas of your life will empower you to feel better, be healthier, and become more productive in every way. And as you've seen in this chapter, it doesn't have to take you a lot of time!

Take some time to reflect on the questions below. Then take out your journal, or download these questions at www.IGiveMyself Permission.com/downloads, and write down your thoughts.

- How do you personally define self-care?

- How well do you routinely take care of yourself? What would you rate yourself in this regard on a scale of 1 to 5, with 5 representing excellent at self-care?

- What negative messages have you heard about self-care? Do you believe them?

- Is it hard for you to give yourself permission to practice self-care? Do you feel guilty when you take time for yourself?

- If you didn't feel guilty, what self-care activities would you indulge in?

- What barriers or challenges keep you from practicing self-care? How do you propose to overcome these obstacles?

- Do you struggle with time for self-care? Can you think of ways to add it to your schedule?

- What self-care techniques do you practice that are on level one (for example, spa, bath, nail salon, day off, watching a movie or TV show)? What techniques do you practice that are deeper and more impactful?

- What feelings did you experience as you read this chapter?

- What are your top five self-care practices? If you don't have five yet, write down the ones you'd like to try.

Chapter 11

I Give Myself Permission to Commit to Myself

To embark on the journey towards your goals and dreams requires bravery. To remain on that path requires courage. The bridge that merges the two is commitment.

—Steve Maraboli

Nine months after the first time I shared my "I Give Myself Permission" talk publicly at a self-care retreat for veterans in Colorado, I found myself at a crossroads. For almost twenty years, I had worked at an outpatient mental health organization, filling various roles, including part-time student, adjunct professor, researcher, interviewer, media personality, assistant program director for a therapy master's program, full-time therapist, brand ambassador, and chief innovation officer. I also witnessed six CEO changes during that time and flirted with the idea of one day becoming the CEO of the organization myself.

At the same time, I built a personal brand and was sought after for media and speaking opportunities. I knew that at some point I would have to decide to either give up my personal brand and move into a new role at the organization or leave it to grow my own brand and personal business.

In moments when I would think about the future, I believed the most likely outcome would involve leaving the organization. But in my daydreams of how it would play out, my departure would happen after a very prominent and possibly lucrative offer that I couldn't refuse. I thought that giving myself permission to launch and leap would be a clear-cut, easy, no-brainer decision. I thought the transition would come in a smooth and seamless way without any challenging emotions. That isn't what happened.

It was two years after the pandemic started. There were many changes to work culture across the world. Opportunities for my personal brand steadily increased, while staying at the organization became more challenging and limiting. But it was scary to think of going full time with my own company and leaving the security of what was comfortable and familiar. If I stayed, I would be frustrated. If I left, I would have to figure things out on my own, and my business might not be successful.

As with any significant decision, I consulted my wife and we talked it through. We also consulted other trusted advisors and mentors. We decided an abrupt departure wouldn't be wise and agreed that giving it another six months would be best, allowing me to leave at the end of the calendar year.

Underneath it all, I had to give myself permission in all the areas I have shared with you in this book. I had to take risks, be okay with an imperfect process, have the courage to live boldly, and much more. All the ways I gave myself permission helped me do something new. I had to give myself permission to take the risk of going full time on my own, face the possibility of my business failing, and lean into living more boldly by putting myself out there and believing in what was possible. I had to give myself permission to not be perfect and to acknowledge that I would learn, grow, and make mistakes. I had to give myself permission to love my wife, my family, and myself by doing what would make me happy and successful. I had to give myself permission to let go of what I had known for almost twenty years and move on to something unfamiliar.

I also had to give myself permission to change my family scripts and believe that I could have a successful business, even after watching family members who had failed in their own business ventures. I had to give myself permission to face the trauma I experienced during my graduate education that left me wondering if I was capable of that level of success. I had to give myself permission to forgive those who caused me harm and tried to impact the forward progress of my career. (In doing so, I realized that their attempts actually set me on the path to embrace and fulfill my potential.) I had to give myself permission to play and rest because trying to give the organization everything while building my personal brand didn't leave time for a lot of self-care. I had to give myself permission to take care of myself because I was giving so much to everyone else but not giving enough to myself. Lastly, I had to give myself permission to commit to myself, my future, my joy, my well-being, my purpose, and fulfillment in my business and personal life.

From my current vantage point, I can now say that choosing to leave was one of the best decisions I've ever made. It provided me with more time, rest, fun, and fulfillment.

It was the cumulative process of giving myself permission in multiple areas that helped me fully launch and not look back. I did a 360-degree permission process, where I examined as many areas as possible in my life to determine where I needed to give myself permission to take the leap. This process helped me be my full self while enjoying the people and things I love. And that's what I want for you. Each area in this book in which you give yourself permission is a window into a different part of your life.

When you examine those parts of your life and give yourself permission, you unlock a part of you that was lost, stuck, or missing. It's more than just saying the words. Giving yourself permission is a self-examination process that can lead you to untapped places in your life, as well as new experiences, deeper connections, greater joy, and a plethora of new and exciting thoughts and feelings. Giving yourself permission is an intentional process. It's a commitment you make to yourself to become your best self.

A Tangible Reminder

After I share the barriers to giving ourselves permission in my "I Give Myself Permission" keynote address, I invite participants to write down what they want to give themselves permission to do. In exchange for accepting my invitation, I give them a bracelet embossed with the words I GIVE MYSELF PERMISSION.

This bracelet is meant to be a tangible reminder of the commitment they made in the moment to actively and intentionally give themselves permission to do or not do something. Even wearing it every day, however, people might not feel the power of that reminder until they really need it. It could happen the same day they hear the talk, later in the week, a month, or six months afterward. But when they feel the reminder, it's important to listen to it.

That's what happened to Charles. He helped fathers with mentorship, parenting conferences, fathering circles, and resource support. One day, he was facilitating a fatherhood group as they watched a video about British sprinter Derek Redmond during the 400-meter semifinals race of the 1992 Olympic Games in Barcelona, Spain. Derek was favored to win it all, but during the middle of the heat, he tore his hamstring. After quickly realizing that his dream of winning an Olympic medal was over, he refocused his efforts on reaching the finish line, instantly setting a new goal. He would push through the pain, disappointment, and heartbreak of the moment to complete his race, limping if he had to, and cross the finish line at the Olympics.

But Derek fell to the ground and started to cry when the excruciating pain set in. Would he be denied his goal to complete the race and cross the finish line? Shortly after that moment, his father, Jim, ran down the stands toward the track, picking Derek up. With Derek secured within his arms, Jim walked with his son to the finish line. Security guards rushed over to try to remove Jim from the track, but he passionately pushed them away. "I'm with my son," he told them. In a heroic moment, Derek and his dad walked and limped to the finish line. It was gut-wrenching and powerful. Everyone in the stands was moved, and everyone who watched the video with Charles felt the impact of the moment.

After the fathers in the group finished the video, Charles said, "I've never had a father fight for me like that. I've never had a father come to my aid." As he was talking, he felt hurt, sadness, shame, and anger rush to his throat, but he wasn't going to let himself express them.

In that moment, however, Charles happened to look down and connect to the I GIVE MYSELF PERMISSION bracelet on his wrist. He remembered that it was okay to feel and express his emotions. He remembered that I had shared in the talk that it's okay to cry, even though he hadn't cried in many years. As a result of that trigger, he proceeded to release the emotions that were in his throat and allowed the tears to come.

It was the first time in a very long time that Charles had given himself permission to have a deep, deep cry. It was meaningful, cleansing, and even necessary for him. Shortly after, he sent me a message saying, "Thank you. I'm grateful to not only have heard you speak but to be reminded to give myself permission through the bracelet."

Charles was honest with the group of fathers. Then he went home and was vulnerable with his wife. He had learned that when we keep our emotions and pain bottled up inside, we can become moody and irritable.

Even though you don't have a bracelet reminding you to give yourself permission, you can create your own trigger as a reminder of your commitment to yourself. It might be a paper clip or rubber band in your pocket. It might be a sign above your desk or your screen-saver. Please don't just read this book without implementing the principles so that you can live your life fully—the life you deserve to have.

Making a Permission Commitment

Finally, as we near the end of the book, let's make a formal "I Give Myself Permission" commitment. First, take a moment to breathe deeply. Think about all the thoughts and feelings that have come up for you throughout the process of reading these chapters. Think about all the ways you want to give yourself permission.

Then repeat the following commitments. You can read them from the book or download them at www.IGiveMyselfPermission. com/downloads. You can say them in front of a mirror or to a trusted person in your life. Say these lines with confidence. As you say each line, think about what it means to you and what you will do to make it a reality. Afterward, I invite you to share your permission stories with me and others at www.IGiveMyselfPermission.com/stories.

I give myself permission to change my negative narratives.

I give myself permission to believe stories about possibilities.

I give myself permission to risk, fail, and live boldly.

I give myself permission to not be perfect.

I give myself permission to love and be loved.

I give myself permission to let go and move on.

I give myself permission to change family scripts.

I give myself permission to face my trauma and heal.

I give myself permission to forgive myself and others.

I give myself permission to play and rest.

I give myself permission to take care of myself.

I give myself permission to feel and express my feelings.

I give myself permission to commit to myself.

I give myself permission to love myself.

I give myself permission to read this book again as much as needed.

I give myself permission to _____.

Wrapping Up

These exercises will strengthen your commitment to giving yourself permission.

- Reflect on what you've learned throughout the book and prioritize the area in your life where you would first like to give yourself more permission. Write down the practical steps you can take to help you get closer to your permission goals.

- Decide on one action to move you toward your goal and develop a timeline that will guide you in completing it.

- On a notepad, write down your commitment, which will serve as a mantra to help you achieve your goal.

- Put your Permission Commitment in a place where you can see it often and be reminded daily. If you like, you can also create a reminder to keep in your pocket; for example, a small, laminated card with your commitment written on it.

- Practice patience as you adopt the new ways you are giving yourself permission.

Acknowledgments

This book would not have been possible without many people helping, supporting, guiding, advocating, believing and championing me before, during, and after the completion of this book.

I am grateful to God for giving me the inspiration for this book, the faith that it will be impactful, the perseverance to see it through, and the ability to do the work I do. Thank you, Mum and Dad. Even though you are not here with me anymore, I can feel you and hear you, especially in this journey. Thank you for your love, prayers, and faith in me. I want to thank my wife, Dr. Candace Robertson-James, who has been by my side since the first time I said I wanted to write a book. Your encouragement, love, ideas, prayers, thought partnership, and edits to this book have been invaluable. Thank you to my children, Nalani and Alex, for constantly providing me joy, light, and inspiration throughout my many endeavors. To my amazing mother-in-law, Diana Robertson, I appreciate your support and how hard you fight for me and those you love. To Joy Jamil, the best executive assistant in the world, you continue to make me and the business better and I appreciate you.

To my agent, Regina Brooks, and the team at Serendipity Literary, thank you for believing in me and connecting me with New Harbinger Publications. To Jed Bickman and the rest of the New Harbinger team, thank you for this opportunity to share my work with the world. I appreciate the many editors who have helped me throughout this process, including Melanie Votaw, Beth Bolton, and Karen Schader.

To all the people whose stories are represented in this book, thank you for trusting me and sharing your life with me. To all the attendees of my "I Give Myself Permission" keynote talks, thank you for what you shared during and after my talk to help me write this book. Thank you to all my mentors, supervisors, professors, supporters, colleagues, peers, students, supervisees, and mentees who have added to my clinical experience and perspective. These people have continuously gone above and beyond to help me throughout my life, and I appreciate you: Rosemary Flowers-Jackson, Mark Johnson, Dr. Phyllis Swint, Dr. Steve Treat, Michael Veloric, Dr. Terry Nance, Dr. Crystal Lucky, Dr. Maghan Keita, Dr. Ed Collymore, Linda Coleman, Dr. Jed Yalof, Dr. Janet Etzi, Trabian Shorters, Rev. David Brown, Dr. James Wadley, Al Chiaradonna, Russ Kilman, Dr. Jeffrey Kudisch, Jennifer Wiess, Jeffrey & Jenifer Westphal, Geoffrey & Gretchen Jackson, Bradley Gayton, and so many others..

To the many people who have been supporters of my work, I thank you. To Leonard Hammonds II, thank you for seeing more in me, my work, and I Give Myself Permission than I was able to see at the time. To all the people who have helped me build my work, brand, thoughts, and experiences to help others give themselves permission, including Dr. Toyo Aboderin, Nichole Harrison, Kenan Etale, Yetunde Shorters, Carlos and Katherine Greene, Kelsey Phariss, Bonnie Benjamin-Phariss, Euan Henry, Katrina Edmonds, Marcus Morales, and SBK Media.

To everyone who has endorsed and championed this book, I am so grateful. Thank you, Jon Gordon bestselling author of *The Energy Bus*, for your friendship, trust, and willingness to share my work. To BJ Johnson, one of my best friends who is constantly an inspiration to me. Thank you, Elizabeth Earnshaw, for sharing how the process works, connecting me with people who led me to one of my editors, and for endorsing the book. Thank you, Leon Ford and Damion Cooper, for allowing me to share your stories. Thanks to my friends and endorsers, three-time NBA champion Danny Green, NBC News anchor and correspondent Savannah Sellers, actor Toney Goins, business strategist and Wharton MBA Lecturer Daria Torres, NYT bestselling author and activist Shaka Senghor, nationally syndicated tech contributor and author Stephanie Humphrey, TV host and relationship expert Paul Brunson, author and television and podcast host Dr. Marc Lamont Hill, and global chief marketing officer for Tinder Melissa Hobley.

To my friends and family who love and believe in me, thank you. I appreciate that no matter what I do or what project I am working on, you are always there for me. Thank you for all those who have prayed for me, introduced me to a new friend, and/or created a new opportunity for me.

Thank you for purchasing this book, reading the book, sharing the book with others, and using the book to give yourself permission.

References

Akimbekov, N. S., and M. S. Razzaque. 2021. "Laughter Therapy: A Humor-Induced Hormonal Intervention to Reduce Stress and Anxiety." *Current Research in Physiology* 4: 135–138.

American Dental Association (ADA). 2021. Health Policy Institute Study. https://www.ada.org/about/press-releases/2021-archives/new-survey-finds-stress-related-dental-conditions-continue-to-increase

American Psychiatric Association. 1968. *Diagnostic and Statistical Manual of Mental Disorders*. 2nd ed. Washington DC: American Psychiatric Association

American Psychological Association. n.d. https://www.apa.org/topics/trauma

———. 2013. "Stress and Sleep." https://www.apa.org/news/press/releases/stress/2013/sleep

———. 2019. "Manage Stress: Strengthen Your Support Network." https://www.apa.org/topics/stress/manage-social-support

Boyatzis, R. E., and A. McKee. 2005. *Resonant Leadership: Renewing Yourself and Connecting with Others Through Mindfulness, Hope, and Compassion*. Boston: Harvard Business School Press.

Centers for Disease Control. 2022. "Leading Causes of Death." https://wisqars.cdc.gov/

Clear, J. 2018. *Atomic Habits: An Easy & Proven Way to Build Good Habits & Break Bad Ones*. New York: Avery Publishing.

Cleveland Clinic. 2021. "How Box Breathing Can Help You Destress." https://health.clevelandclinic.org/box-breathing-benefits

Curran, T., and A. P. Hill. 2019. "Perfectionism Is Increasing Over Time: A Meta-Analysis of Birth Cohort Differences from 1989 to 2016." *Psychological Bulletin* 145 (4): 410–429.

Duhigg, C. 2012. *The Power of Habit: Why We Do What We Do in Life and Business.* New York: Random House.

Ford, L. 2023. *An Unspeakable Hope: Brutality, Forgiveness, and Building a Better Future for My Son.* New York: Atria Books.

Freud, S. 1896. *The Aetiology of Hysteria.*

———. 1997. *The Interpretation of Dreams.* Translated by A. A. Brill. Knoxville, TN: Wordsworth Editions.

Gibson, J. 2025. "Remittance: What It Is and How to Send One." https://www.investopedia.com/terms/r/remittance.asp

Ginwright, S. 2022. *The Four Pivots: Reimagining Justice, Reimagining Ourselves.* Berkeley, CA: North Atlantic Books.

Harvard Medical School. "National Comorbidity Survey 2001–2003." https://www.hcp.med.harvard.edu/ncs

Herman, J. 1997. *Trauma and Recovery: The Aftermath of Violence— From Domestic Abuse to Political Terror.* New York: Basic Books.

James, G. 2020. "Racial Trauma and Ways to Cope." https://www. theconsciouskid.org/racial-trauma

Jordan, M. J. 2009. Naismith National Basketball Association Hall of Fame Induction Speech.

Jung, C. G. 2003. *Psychology of the Unconscious.* Garden City, NY: Dover Publications.

Kerr, M. E., and M. Bowen. 1988. *Family Evaluation.* New York: W. W. Norton & Company.

King, M. L., Jr. 2018. Letter from Birmingham Jail. Penguin Classics.

Lyles, N. 2024. X (formerly Twitter) post. https://x.com/LylesNoah

Michaelis, D. 2020. *Eleanor.* New York: Simon & Schuster.

National Heart, Lung and Blood Institute. 2022. "Sleep Deprivation and Deficiency: How Sleep Affects Your Health." https://www.nhlbi.nih.gov/health/sleep-deprivation/health-effects

Olympics. n.d. "Derek Redmond's Emotional Olympic Story: Injury Mid-Race, Barcelona 1992 Olympics." https://www.youtube.com/watch?v=t2G8KVzTwfw

Phoenix, O. 2013. "The Self-Care Wheel (Image)." https://olgaphoenix.com/self-care-wheel

Rowling, J. K. 1998. *Harry Potter and the Sorcerer's Stone.* New York: Scholastic.

———. 2007. *Harry Potter and the Deadly Hallows.* New York: Scholastic.

Swider, B., D. Harari, A. P. Breidenthal, and L. B. Steed. 2018. "The Pros and Cons of Perfectionism According to Research." *Harvard Business Review.* https://hbr.org/2018/12/the-pros-and-cons-of-perfectionism-according-to-research

White, M., and D. Epston. 1990. *Narrative Means to Therapeutic Ends.* New York: W. W. Norton & Company.

World Health Organization. 2024. "Post-Traumatic Stress Disorder." https://www.who.int/news-room/fact-sheets/detail/post-traumatic-stress-disorder

About the Author

George James, **PsyD**, **LMFT**, is the CEO of George Talks, and a licensed therapist, executive coach, international speaker, and corporate consultant with more than twenty years of experience. Known for his expert insights on relationships, mental health, and leadership, Dr. James has been featured on the *Today* show, CBS *Mornings*, CNN, NBC *News Now*, and in *The New York Times*.

His work has been recognized with honors such as the Excellence in Media Award from the American Association of Marriage and Family Therapists, and the BMe Genius Award. A Villanova presidential scholar, Dr. James completed his studies at the university, and returned for his MBA, and lives in the Philadelphia metropolitan area with his wife, Dr. Candace Robertson-James, and their two children, Nalani and Alex.

Real change *is* possible

For more than fifty years, New Harbinger has published proven-effective self-help books and pioneering workbooks to help readers of all ages and backgrounds improve mental health and well-being, and achieve lasting personal growth. In addition, our spirituality books offer profound guidance for deepening awareness and cultivating healing, self-discovery, and fulfillment.

Founded by psychologist Matthew McKay and Patrick Fanning, New Harbinger is proud to be an independent, employee-owned company. Our books reflect our core values of integrity, innovation, commitment, sustainability, compassion, and trust. Written by leaders in the field and recommended by therapists worldwide, New Harbinger books are practical, accessible, and provide real tools for real change.

newharbingerpublications

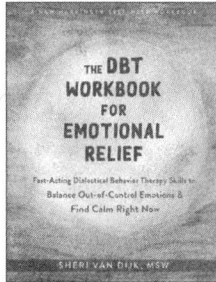

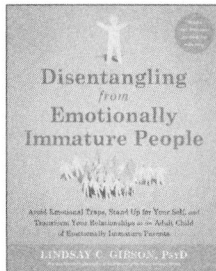

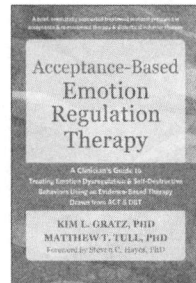